JN492434

A 5-Star Guide to Restaurant & Hotel English

Practical Restaurant & Hotel English

Myeong-Hee Seong

BAEKSAN Publishing

CONTENTS

CHAPTER 1

RESTAURANT SERVICES

Unit 1

Reservations & Receptions

Introduction to the Job Field

Reading 1: Food and Beverage Service

Food services are a feature of hotels. The typical modern hotel includes a restaurant, a coffee shop for quicker and less expensive meals, and a bar or cocktail lounge. Hotels also normally provide room service - food and drink that are brought to the guest's room. In addition, catering service is usually provided in the hotel's recreational areas. The poolside bar and snack bar, for quicker food, are normal parts of the service at a resort hotel.

One of the most important incomes of the hotel is from the sales of food and beverage. The restaurant must create an enjoyable and relaxed ambience for all guests. The guests should enjoy their meals and drinks in the most comfortable way. There are many kinds of staff in the food area: waiters and waitress, head waiters, hostesses, captains, or bus persons. Bus persons help the waiters and waitresses as implied by their name. Not only do they clear dirty dishes, but they also serve guests in many ways. They serve bread, rolls, coffee, and other items. They also set up the tables, change table cloths, clean the floor, fill water glasses, and replenish silverware. Otherwise these would be the waiter or waitress's function, so their work increases the overall efficiency of the service staff. Every restaurant personnel must be courteous, helpful, sales-minded, and fast in service. They should know the menu in detail and make it a daily habit to check the special of the day.

Reading 2: Greeting & Seating the Guest

When entering a restaurant there is usually a greeter (sometimes called a host or hostess) who leads people to their seats and gives them their menus. In some cases, it is necessary for the guests to make reservations in advance. If there is no greeter in the restaurant, then there will be a sign telling the guests to wait to be seated and a waiter will lead them to their tables in the order in which they arrive.

For many customers, waiting for service is a negative experience. Not only Koreans but also foreigners don't like to wait in front of restaurants to have a meal. Thus, speed of service is increasingly becoming a very important service factor even though it is very difficult to control waiting time. You might be in trouble because you can't control the actual wait duration; However, you can control the customer's perception of it.

While procedure may vary from operation to operation, the following sequence will cover most situations:

(1) Promptly acknowledge the guests and welcome them with a greeting. An example of this may be: "Good morning, welcome to Shilla Hotel."
(2) Establish if the customer has a reservation. If customers don't have a reservation, the service staff must make sure that there is a table available. If the guests have a reservation, service staff should check the

number of expected quests for the table.

(3) Show guests to their table.

(4) At the table, pull out one chair to signal to the guests that they are free to claim a seat and sit.

Prep. for Conversation

Vocabulary 1: Types of Meal

Match each word in the first column with its meaning in the second column.

(1) a la carte •	• ⓐ 정식
(2) table d'hote •	• ⓑ 일품요리
(3) dumpling •	• ⓒ 국수
(4) noodles •	• ⓓ 만두
(5) American breakfast •	• ⓔ 돈가스
(6) continental breakfast •	• ⓕ 비프가스
(7) beef cutlet •	• ⓖ 오므라이스
(8) rice omelet •	• ⓗ 달걀 요리가 없이 커피, 빵, 주스 정도의 간단한 식사
(9) pork cutlet •	• ⓘ 달걀 요리를 중심으로 하여 주스 혹은 과일, 시리얼, 빵, 소시지, 커피로 구성되는 아침식사

Vocabulary 2: Table Setting

(10) set up the tables •	• ⓙ 은식기를 보충하다
(11) fill water glasses •	• ⓚ 식탁보를 갈다
(12) change table cloths •	• ⓛ 물 컵을 채우다
(13) replenish silverware •	• ⓜ 상을 차리다

Key Expressions: Reservations & Seating the Guest

How can you say the following in English?

1. 6명 식사 좀 예약합니다.

(a table, I'd like, reserve, to, 6, for)

2. 예약은 최소한 하루 전에 해주시면 좋겠습니다.

(to make, your reservation, in advance, at least, one day, it's, good)

3. 어느 분 성함으로 예약해 드릴까요?

(shall, make, I, the reservation, what name, in, ?)

4. 죄송합니다. 오늘은 예약이 완료되어 좌석이 없습니다.

(I'm sorry, fully, we're, booked)

5. 창가 자리를 주세요.

(the window, by, a table, I, want)

6. 예약을 하셨습니까?

(you, a reservation, have, do, ?)

7. 얼마나 오래 기다려야 합니까?

(how long, is, there, a wait, of, ?)

8. 약 10분을 기다려야 합니다.

....

(about, 10 minutes, to wait, there are)

9. 테이블이 준비되면 이름을 부르겠습니다.

....

(your table, is ready, when, I'll, you, call)

10. 이 자리가 마음에 드십니까?

....

(this table, you, like, do, how, ?)

Practice Makes Perfect

Conversation 1 Calling to Book for Lunch

C : Captain G : Guest

C : Good morning. Seasons Restaurant, Mr. Lee speaking.
How can I help you?

G : I'm calling to book for lunch tomorrow.

C : For what time and for how many would that be, sir?

G : I'd like to book a table for five at one o'clock.

C : Fine! Who's booking, sir?

G : Bill Jones.

C : Thank you, Mr. Jones. We'll reserve a table for five at 1:00 p.m. tomorrow.

G : Thank you. Bye.

Conversation 2 Making a Reservation for Dinner

M : Manager G : Guest

M : Rainbow Restaurant, may I help you?

G : I've got a group of 15 people. We want to make a reservation for dinner tomorrow at your restaurant.

M : Very well. May I have your name, sir?

G : Jonathan Thomas.

M : What time would you like the reservation, Mr. Thomas?

G : We'll be there at around 7:00 p.m.

M : That's good, Mr. Thomas. May I have your telephone number, please?

G : Yes, my phone number is 751-8104. We want tables near the window with a nice view.

M : We'll have the tables by the window ready for you.

G : Thank you.

M : If you'd like to change or cancel, please call us, Mr. Thomas.

G : Sure.

M : Thank you for calling us.

Conversation 3 Cancelling the Reservation

Ⓜ : Manager Ⓖ : Guest

G : Is this the Rose Restaurant?

M : Yes, sir. May I help you?

G : Yes. I'm very sorry. I made a reservation for a table for three for dinner tomorrow at 7:00, but I have to cancel my reservation. My plans changed.

M : Who made the reservation, sir?

G : Mr. Cooper.

M : Thanks for letting us know. I hope we may serve you next time.

G : I hope so, too. Goodbye.

Conversation 4 Booking a Table for the Lunch Buffet

Ⓡ : Receptionist Ⓖ : Guest

R : Hello, Rose Garden Buffet, Hyatt. Miss Hong speaking. May I help you?

G : Yes, may I know what time you serve the dinner buffet?

R : Of course, sir. We serve dinner only on Sundays from 6 p.m. to 9:30 p.m.

G : Only Sundays?

R : Yes, sir.

G : I see. How about the lunch buffet?

R : We serve the lunch buffet from noon to 2:30 p.m. 7 days a week, sir.

G : OK. Can I book a table for the lunch buffet for 6 this coming Saturday?

R : Saturday, April twelfth……. Yes. Smoking or nonsmoking, sir?

G : Nonsmoking, please.

R : What time would you like, sir?

G : 12:30, please. I'm going to reserve it under my name, Mr. Hopkins.

R : OK. A nonsmoking table for 6 on Saturday, April 12 at 12:30 p.m. under Mr. Hopkins. Is that correct, Mr. Hopkins?

G : Yes, exactly.

R : Where could I contact you, Mr. Hopkins?

G : My phone number's 503-7704.

R : 503-7704. Anything else, Mr. Hopkins?

G : No, that's all. Thank you.

R : Thank you for calling, Mr. Hopkins. See you on Saturday. Goodbye.

Conversation 5 Reserving a Table for Three

Ⓜ : Manager Ⓖ : Guest

M : Good morning, River View. May I help you?

G : Yes, please. What time do you open for dinner?

M : We are open from 6:00 to 10:00 p.m. sir.

G : I'd like to reserve a table for three for this evening.

M : For this evening, and for what time would that be, sir?

G : We'll be there at about 6:30.

M : May I have your name, please?

G : My name is Jack Martin.

M : We will reserve your table for 6:30, Mr. Martin.

G : That's great.

M : Thank you for calling. We'll be expecting you, Mr. Martin.

G : Thank you. Bye.

Conversation 6 Guest without Reservation

Ⓡ : Receptionist Ⓖ : Guest

R : Good afternoon, sir. How are you today?

G : Just fine. Do you have a table for three?

R : Did you make a reservation, sir?

G : No, we didn't.

R : I'm sorry, sir. We don't have any tables available at the moment. If you don't mind waiting, we can make a table for you in about 10 minutes, sir.

G : That sounds great. We'll wait here.

R : Would you like smoking or nonsmoking, sir?

G : Nonsmoking, please.

R : I'll have a table ready as soon as possible.

(Later)

Your table is ready now, sir. We're very sorry for having kept you so long. I'll show you to your table. Would you please follow me, sir?

G : Can we have that table by the window?

R : Oh, I'm sorry. That table is reserved, but here's a nice table for three.

G : That's fine. I appreciate your kindness.

R : Your server will be right with you. Here's your menu.

Conversation 7 Guest with Reservation

Ⓡ : Receptionist Ⓖ : Guest

R : How are you this evening, sir?

G : I'm just great.

R : Did you make a reservation?

G : Yes, a table for two at 7:30. The name is Robinson.

R : Would you come this way, please?

How do you like this table?

G : That would be great.

R : I'll be right back in a moment, sir.

Conversation 8 No Tables Left

Ⓗ : Hostess Ⓖ : Guest

H : How many?

G : Two.

H : There are no tables left for two at this moment. Could you wait?

G : Yes. How long of a wait is there?

H : About 30 minutes. We are going to get a couple of free tables soon.
I'll call you just as soon as we are ready.

Conversation 9 Table by the Window

Ⓗ : Hostess Ⓖ : Guest

H : Did you make a reservation, sir?

G : Yes, I'm John Kim. I reserved a table for two.

H : Yes, Mr. Kim. A party of two. Come this way.
Is this table all right?

G : I don't like a booth.
Do you by any chance have a table near the window?

H : I'm afraid we don't.

Conversation 10 Guest without Reservation

Ⓡ : Receptionist Ⓖ : Guest

R : Good evening. May I help you?

G : Hello. Do you have a table for two now?

R : By the way, sir. Do you have a reservation?

G : No, we just arrived in here.

R : I'm sorry, the reservation is full at this moment, but we can make a table for you in about half an hour. Would it be possible to wait for a while, sir?

G : O.K.

R : Why don't you have a seat in the lounge, and we will let you know when the table is ready.

G : All right, my name is Smith.

Practice Point

Complete the following conversations relating to the previous Conversations.

1

Guest : I'm calling to (   ) for lunch tomorrow.

Captain : For what time and (   ) how many would that be, sir?

2

Guest : We want tables near the window with a nice view.

Manager : We'll have the table by the window (   ) for you.

3

Guest : I have to cancel my reservation. My plans changed.

Manager : Who (   ) the reservation, sir?

4

Receptionist : We (   ) dinner only on Sundays from 6 p.m. to 9 p.m.

Guest : Only Sundays?

5

Guest : What time do you open for dinner?

Manager : We are (   ) from 6:00 to 10:00 p.m., sir.

6

Receptionist : We don't have any tables (   ) at the moment. If you don't mind (   ), we can make a table for you in about 10 minutes, sir.

Guest : That sounds great.

7

Receptionist : Would you come this way, please?

Guest : (   ) would be great.

8

Hostess : How (   ) ?

Guest : Two.

9

Guest : I don't like a booth. Do you by any (   ) have a table near the window?

Hostess : I'm afraid we don't.

Unit 2

Breakfast & Lunch Services

Introduction to the Job Field

Reading 1: Hotel Breakfast

The types of hotel breakfasts are the continental breakfast, American breakfast, Japanese breakfast, Korean breakfast, etc. There are also a wide variety of a la carte dishes: juices, pancakes, toast or eggs.

The American breakfast, popular with businessmen, is not confined to Americans. Generally speaking, the American breakfast consists of fruit juice, potato and two eggs, some bacon, ham or sausage, and coffee or tea. But its exact elements depend upon location.

The continental breakfast is also popular with business people. It is a light but sufficient breakfast. The continental breakfast does not include potatoes and eggs as in the American breakfast. It is typically eaten in European countries, especially France and Italy, and it consists of croissants or bread rolls, butter, jam, and coffee.

The oriental breakfast refers chiefly to the Korean or Japanese breakfast. In general, it does not include Chinese meals. These meals normally consist of light dishes which do not burden the stomach. The Japanese breakfast typically consists of a bowl of rice, a bowl of miso soup (Japanese bean paste soup), a raw egg mixed with soy sauce, a piece of fried fish and a few pickled vegetables. The Korean breakfast has not been yet standardized but it is often classified according to the types of soup. These breakfast soups include: beef turnip, bean sprout, seaweed, and Haejang-guk. In addition, a bowl of rice and side-dishes are served, i.e., some kimchi, bulgogi, dried seaweed, fried fish and others.

Reading 2: Business Luncheon

The business luncheon of hotels is a lunch served quickly for business people consisting of 2 or 3 courses, neither, too rich nor too simple. It was developed by deluxe hotel restaurants and other quality restaurants. For this type of lunch, soups vary restaurant by restaurant; they are also served differently on a daily basis under the name of 'soup of the day.' It is often made with ingredients in season.

Prep. for Conversation

Vocabulary: Types of Cooked Eggs

Match each word in the first column with its meaning in the second column.

＊Fried Egg

(1) sunny-side up	•	• ⓐ 한 면만 반숙 프라이한 계란
(2) turned over	•	• ⓑ 양면을 프라이한 계란
(3) over easy	•	• ⓒ 양면을 살짝 프라이 한 계란

＊Boiled Egg

(4) soft boiled egg	•	• ⓓ 흰자만 익힌 삶은 계란
(5) hard boiled egg	•	• ⓔ 노른자까지 익힌 삶은 계란
(6) poached egg	•	• ⓕ 저어서 풀어 볶은 계란
(7) scrambled egg	•	• ⓖ 수란(깨어서 끓는 물에 떨어뜨려 삶은 계란)

＊Eggs are ____________________________________.

(8) raw	•	• ⓗ 날 것 그대로입니다.
(9) runny	•	• ⓘ 익어서 흐물거려요.
(10) undercooked	•	• ⓙ 덜 익었어요.
(11) overcooked	•	• ⓚ 너무 익었어요.
(12) soft	•	• ⓛ 단단해요.
(13) hard	•	• ⓜ 익지 않아서 반숙 상태입니다.

Key Expressions: Hotel Breakfast & Lunch Services

How can you say the following in English?

1. 주문 받을까요?

....

(I, your order, take, now, may, ?)

2. 오늘 아침 메뉴에는 무엇이 좋습니까?

....

(this morning, the menu, on, what's, good, ?)

3. 토스트는 바싹 구울까요, 살짝 구울까요?

....

(your toast, dark, or, light, how, you, would, like, ?)

4. 빨리 갖다 주세요. 시간이 없습니다.

....

(Please, my order, rush, I, don't, much, time, have)

5. 달걀 어떻게 해드릴까요?

....

(your eggs, how, you, like, would, ?)

6. 스파게티는 메뉴에 없습니다.

....

(Spaghetti, the menu, on, is, not)

7. 당근이 덜 익었습니다.

....

(The carrots, enough, not, are, cooked)

8. 제일 먼저 무엇을 드시겠습니까?

....

(start, with, what, would, like to, you, ?)

9. 그 다음엔 무엇을 드시겠습니까?

....

(and, you, what, follow, to, would, like, ?)

10. 후식은 무엇으로 하시겠습니까?

....

(for dessert, you, what, would, like, ?)

Practice Makes Perfect

Conversation 1 I'd like the American Breakfast.

Ⓦ : Waiter Ⓖ : Guest

W : Good morning, gentlemen.

G : Good morning.

W : Would you like to see the menu?

G : No, thanks. We're ready to order.

W : Good. What would you like, gentlemen?

G1 : I'd like the American breakfast, please.

W : Very good. What kind of juice would you like, sir?

G1 : Tomato juice, please.

W : How would you like the two eggs?

G1 : Fried, please.

W : We can make the fried eggs sunny-side-up, over-easy, over-medium, over-well (over-hard).

G1 : Over-easy, please. And do side dishes come with the eggs?

W : You may have potatoes and bacon, ham or sausages. You have a choice of meat.

G1 : I'll have the ham. How about bread? Do you also serve bread with the egg dishes?

W : Yes, sir. We normally serve toast with the eggs. But we also serve other breads if you request.

G1 : The toast is fine with me.

W : Would you like some coffee or tea to follow?

G1 : Decafe for me, please.

W : Decaffeinated coffee, very good, sir.

(The waiter turns to the other gentleman.)

What would you like, sir?

G2 : I'll have the same, but scrambled eggs only.

W : How would you like your scrambled eggs, soft or hard, sir?

G2 : Soft. And with some sausages, please. Could we start with the drinks? Green tea for me.

W : Certainly. The beverages will be served immediately and the egg dishes will be served in 5 minutes. Thank you for the orders.

Conversation 2 We'll Take the Continental Breakfast.

Ⓦ : Waiter Ⓖ : Guest

W : Good morning.

G : Good morning.

W : Would you like some coffee or tea before you order?

G : That's great.

G1 : I will have coffee, please.

G2 : I'll have hot chocolate, please.

W : May I show you the menu, sir?

G : No, it's not necessary. We will take the continental breakfast.

W : Very good, sir. Which juice would you like, sir?

G1 : Tomato juice for me and grapefruit juice for my friend, please.

W : How about the bread, sir?

G1 : I will have the rye bread, please.

W : Would you like your bread toasted?

G1 : Yes, I would like it dark too.

W : How about yours, sir?

G2 : What other breads and pastries do you have?

W : Well, we have Croissants, Donuts, Danish Pastries, Sweet Rolls, English Muffins, and various fruit muffins.

G2 : Sounds great. Can I have a basket of all assorted.

W : Sure, sir.

G2 : Do we have to order the jams for breads?

W : No, it's not necessary. Jams, marmalades and butter always accompany the bread.

G1 : Do you also provide any English newspapers in the morning?

W : Yes, we have the Korea Times, and I will have the bellboy bring the papers to you immediately. Anything else, sir?

G : That's it.

W : Thank you very much. Your orders will be ready in a couple of minutes.

Conversation 3 One Korean & One Japanese Breakfast

Ⓦ : Waiter Ⓖ : Guest

W : Good morning. How are you this morning?

G : Very good. Thanks.

W : There you are, sir. We have the teas here, the green tea for "The Japanese Breakfast", and the barley tea for "The Korean Breakfast".

G : Can we have a choice for drinks?

W : Certainly, sir, and tea is complimentary.

G1 : That's great. I'll have the Korean Breakfast, please.

G2 : I'll have the Japanese breakfast, please.

(The waiter writes down on the order pad, repeating to himself.)

W : One Korean breakfast and one Japanese breakfast. Very good, sir.

G : Excuse me. By the way, we know the Korean breakfast well. But what do you normally serve for the Japanese breakfast?

W : Well, every restaurant serves the Japanese breakfast in a slightly different way. But our Japanese breakfast consists of a bowl of rice with an egg mixed in soy sauce, a bowl of Miso soup, a piece of fried fish, a few pickles, and green tea. It's served on a tray.

G2 : That's fine with me. I'll take it.

G1 : How about the Korean breakfast here in this restaurant?

W : Well, we normally have three different soups in the morning. Beef turnip soup, bean sprout soup and Haejang-guk. But today's Korean breakfast is served with a bowl of beef turnip soup, a bowl of rice, some kimchi, some bulgogi and some dried seaweed with soy sauce.

Conversation 4 What Would You Like To Start With?

Ⓦ : Waiter Ⓖ : Guest

W : Good morning, ma'am. Good morning, sir.

G : Good morning.

W : Would you like to see the menu?

G : Yes, please.

W : Here you are.

(A few minutes later . . . the waiter returns.)

W : Are you ready to order?

G1 : Oh, yes. We are ready, I guess.

W : What would you like to start with?

G1 : One coffee and a glass of orange juice, please.

(The waiter makes a note and repeats.)

W : A cup of coffee and a glass of orange juice.

G1 : And a bowl of corn flakes with some strawberries. And with a pastry to follow, please.

W : All right ma'am. Is there anything else?

G1 : No, that's all for me.

W : How about you, sir?

G2 : I'll have a cup of tea and a glass of grapefruit juice, please.

W : All right, sir. What else would you like, sir?

G2 : Well, I'll have the French toast with some bacon, please.

Please, don't forget to bring maple syrup with the French toast.

W : Certainly, sir.

Conversation 5 I'll Have the American Breakfast

Ⓦ : Waiter Ⓖ : Guest

W : Good morning, sir. Are you ready to order now?

G : Yes, I'll have this American breakfast combination.

W : OK, sir. What kind of juice would you like?

You have a choice of orange, grapefruit, or tomato juice.

G : I'll have tomato juice.

W : OK, tomato. Next, you get two eggs cooked as you wish.

G : Sunny-side up, please.

W : OK, sunny-side up, and you have a choice of sausage links or bacon.

G : I'll take bacon. Make sure it's good and crisp!

W : Yes, sir, crisp bacon.

Next, you have a choice of hash-brown potatoes or cereal.

G : What sorts of cereals do you have?

W : We have cold cereals such as corn flakes, shredded wheat, and puffed rice, and also hot cereals such as oatmeal and cream of wheat.

G : Cream of wheat, then. And make my toast light.

W : Yes, sir. Coffee or tea?

G : A cup of coffee, please, with sugar but no cream.

W : OK. I'll bring your order right away.

Conversation 6 Bring me a Hamburger

Ⓦ : Waiter Ⓖ : Guest

W : Are you ready to order your lunch?

G : Yes. Bring me a hamburger but hold the onions.

W : What would you like to drink?

G : Do you have diet coke?

W : No, we don't. We have diet 7-up, though.

G : A large diet 7-up with lots of ice.

Conversation 7 Ready to Order Now, Sir?

Ⓦ : Waiter Ⓖ : Guest

W : Would you care for a cocktail before your lunch?

G : Yes. Vodka martini, please.

W : Ready to order now, sir?

G : Fillet mignon with rice.

W : How do you want your steak?

G : Medium, please.

Conversation 8 Let Me Have a Large Coke.

Ⓦ : Waiter Ⓖ : Guest

W : Are you ready to order, sir?

G : Yes. I'll have a B.L.T sandwich.

W : Would you like to order something to drink?

G : Yes, let me have a large coke.

Conversation 9 I'll Have the Business Luncheon.

Ⓡ : Receptionist Ⓖ : Guest Ⓦ : Waiter

R : Good afternoon, gentlemen. Do you have a reservation?

G : No, we don't. Do you have room for two?

R : Luckily, we have a couple of tables available. One is near the window and the other is in the corner. Where do you prefer, sir?

G : By the window, please.

(The receptionist shows the guests to the table.)

R : Here we are and here are the menus, sir. Your waiter will be with you in a minute. He will be glad to assist you in ordering.

G : Thanks.

W : Good afternoon. I am your waiter, sir. May I help you?

G1 : What is the "Business Luncheon" here?

W : We normally have two Business Luncheons every day. So, you have a choice.

G2 : Could you recommend one for us?

W : They're both excellent. You won't be disappointed.

G1 : Can you tell us more about this one?

W : The Business Luncheon No. 1 is the Veal Cordon Bleu which is a typical French dish made of sliced and breaded veal, stuffed with ham and cheese, and pan-fried. And the No. 2 is the Sole Meunire, also in the typical French style. It's very popular here. The same soup and salad of the day come with each.

G2 : Sounds great. I think I'll have the No.1, please. How about you, John?

G1 : Excellent. I'll have the same. Waiter! We'll have the No.1 for two, please.

W : Thank you, sir.

Practice Point

Complete the following conversations relating to the previous Conversations.

1

Waiter : (   ) would you like the two eggs?

Guest : Fried, please.

2

Guest : Do we have to order the jams for breads?

Waiter : No, it's not necessary. Jam, marmalades and butter always (   ) the bread.

3

Waiter : We have the green tea for "the Japanese Breakfast," and the barley tea for "the (   ) breakfast".

Guest : Can we have a choice for dinner?

4

Waiter : What would you like to start (   )?

Guest : One coffee and a glass of orange juice, please.

5

Guest : A cup of coffee, please, with sugar but no (   ).

Waiter : O.K. I'll bring your order right away.

6

Waiter : Are you ready to order your lunch?

Guest : Bring me a hamburger but (   ) the onions.

7

Waiter : (   ) do you like your steak?

Guest : Medium, please.

8

Waiter : Are you (   ) to order?

Guest : Yes. I'll have a B.L.T sandwich.

9

Guest 1 : Sounds great. I'll have the No. 1, please.

Guest 2 : Excellent. I'll have the (   ).

Unit 3

Dinner Service

Introduction to the Job Field

Reading 1: Table Setting

Table setting is an essential preparatory process. It is especially important in Western restaurant service. The formality and types of the table setting can be differentiated according to the types and characteristics of the meal: breakfast, luncheon, dinner, party and others. For speed and accuracy, how to set the table, along with its English expressions and terms, should be learned. Rules for setting table are followings.

- Side plates should always be placed to the left of the fork.
- Knife blades should always face left.
- Sufficient space should be left between the knife and fork for the meal to be placed down (approximately 25-30cm depending on the size and shape of the main course plate).
- Entree cutlery should always be placed on the outside of the main cutlery.

- In a la carte dining, the dessert cutlery should be placed where the main knife is usually positioned.
- Wine glass should be placed directly above the main knife.

Reading 2: Order Taking

The key to your success as a waiter or waitress is salesmanship at the moment you take the order. You have the responsibility every time you take an order to help your guests select foods and beverages.

(1) Know Your Menu First

You should make it a daily habit to check the special of the menu, and to note any changes in the items listed. Please find out what the ingredients of different dishes are and how long they take to prepare.

(2) Help Your Guest Through Suggestive Selling

Try to analyze the average guest and find out what influences their choice of items. You can take it for granted they are not dieting or allergic to anything.

(3) Make Your Suggestion Colorful But Specific

Name only two items to give your guest an easy choice. It's easier to decide between two items than to pick from five or six.

Prep. for Conversation

Vocabulary 1: Steak

Match each word in the first column with its meaning in the second column.

(1) filet mignon	ⓐ 쇠고기 안심 스테이크
(2) sirloin steak	ⓑ 소 넓적다리살 스테이크
(3) rib steak	ⓒ 소 옆구리살로 만든 스테이크
(4) flank steak	ⓓ 소갈비 스테이크
(5) T-bone steak	ⓔ 소 등뼈가 붙어있는 고기부분의 스테이크
(6) round steak	ⓕ 소 허리고기 윗부분의 스테이크(등심스테이크)
(7) rump steak	ⓖ 소 엉덩잇살 스테이크
(8) tenderloin steak	ⓗ 안심 스테이크의 일종으로 소의 두텁고 부드러운 허리고기로 만든 스테이크
(9) rare	ⓘ 조금 태운 상태
(10) medium	ⓙ 잘 익은 상태
(11) well-done	ⓚ 완전히 익지 않고 설익은 상태
(12) burnt	ⓛ 알맞게 익은 상태

Vocabulary 2: Salad & Dressings

Match each word in the first column with its meaning in the second column.

*Simple Salad(순수한 채소로만 구성되는 샐러드)

(1) green salad • • ⓐ 여러 가지 채소를 혼합하여 만든 샐러드
(2) leaf salad • • ⓑ 순수한 그린색으로 구성된 채소샐러드
(3) vegetable salad • • ⓒ 먹을 수 있는 잎으로 구성된 채소샐러드

*Combined Salad(여러 가지 채소와 함께 과일·생선·육류·조류 등이 혼합된 샐러드)

(4) fruit salad • • ⓓ 채소와 함께 과일이 제공되는 샐러드
(5) fish salad • • ⓔ 채소와 함께 육류가 제공되는 샐러드
(6) meat salad • • ⓕ 채소와 함께 생선이 제공되는 샐러드
(7) poultry salad • • ⓖ 채소와 함께 조류가 제공되는 샐러드

*Dressings

(8) French dressing • • ⓗ 마요네즈에 칠리소스나 토마토케첩을 넣고 피클 등으로 다져넣은 드레싱의 일종
(9) Italian dressing • • ⓘ 오일, 식초, 레몬주스, 양파 등을 섞어 만든 샐러드 드레싱
(10) Ranch dressing • • ⓙ 마요네즈와 버터밀크를 섞어 만든 흰색의 드레싱
(11) Thousand island dressing • • ⓚ 프렌치타입의 드레싱으로 비네그레트소스라고도 함
(12) Honey Mustard • • ⓛ 마요네즈와 겨자가 주재료인 드레싱

Vocabulary 3: Seafood

Match each word in the first column with its meaning in the second column.

(1) seaweed	•	• ⓐ 송어
(2) trout	•	• ⓑ 해초
(3) caviar	•	• ⓒ 갑오징어
(4) cuttlefish	•	• ⓓ 철갑상어 알젓
(5) salmon	•	• ⓔ 참치
(6) tuna	•	• ⓕ 연어
(7) lobster	•	• ⓖ 조개, 대합
(8) flounder	•	• ⓗ 바다가재
(9) clam	•	• ⓘ 가자미
(10) crab	•	• ⓙ 말려서 먹는 오징어
(11) shrimp	•	• ⓚ 게
(12) eel	•	• ⓛ 뱀장어
(13) squid	•	• ⓜ 굴
(14) oyster	•	• ⓝ 새우

Key Expressions: Dinner Service

How can you say the following in English?

1. 스테이크를 어떻게 구워드릴까요?

....

(your steak, how, would, like, you, ?)

2. 스테이크 맛있었습니까?

....

(you, the steak, all right, find, did, ?)

3. 스테이크가 좀 너무 (덜) 구워졌습니다.

(This steak, a little bit, overdone(undercooked), is)

4. 그것은 숯불에서 구웠습니다.

(It's, a charcoal fire, over, grilled)

5. 제가 주문한 것 어떻게 됐습니까?

(my order, what's, happened, to, ?)

6. 기다리시게 해서 죄송합니다.

(I'm sorry, you, have kept, waiting, to)

7. 주문하신 것 곧 나옵니다.

(your order, in a minute, here, will, be)

8. 식사와 곁들여 드시겠습니까?

(your dinner, with, them, have, you, will, ?)

9. 더 익혀 드리겠습니다.

(I'll, it, cooked, have, some more, you, for)

10. 시저 샐러드를 추천하고 싶습니다.

(I'd like, the Caesar salad, to recommend)

Practice Makes Perfect

Conversation 1 What's Good On the Menu Today?

W : Waiter B : Mrs. Brown

W : Good evening, ma'am. May I take your order?

B : Yes. May I have the menu?

W : Yes, ma'am. Here you are.

B : What's good on the menu today?

W : We are selling a lot of sole and flounder tonight. We have them baked or broiled.

B : I'm not too strong on fish. I'll just have a well-done steak.

W : Yes, ma'am. Would you like a baked potato or French fries?

B : A baked potato with sour cream and French dressing on my salad.

W : Thank you for your order.

Conversation 2 I Can Hardly Decide What To Order.

W : Waiter A : Mr. Anderson

W : Good evening, sir. May I take your order?

A : Can I have a menu, please?

W : Yes, sir. Here it is.

A : There is so much on this menu that I can hardly decide what to order.

W : The á la carte dishes are on the left-hand page and the table d'hôte dishes are on the right-hand page, sir.

A : Is there any special dish you would recommend?

W : We have several good chicken dishes, if you like, sir.

A : I'm not fond of chicken.

W : How about seafood, sir? Seafood is one of our chef's best dishes. We have baked salmon and sole.

A : What is this steak on the menu?

W : It's a minced steak cooked over a grill, sir. Of course, it's neither porterhouse nor tenderloin steak. It's a steak, though. I believe it must be a cut of round steak.

A : I think I'll try that. For vegetables, please bring me grilled corn and a baked potato.

W : How would you like your steak, sir?

A : Medium-rare, please. What salad comes with the steak?

W : You have a choice of either lettuce and tomato or beet and cucumber. And you also have a choice of appetizers and soups, sir.

A : Where are the appetizers on the menu, waiter?

W : They are at the top of this page, sir. You can have shrimp cocktail, fresh fruit cocktail, tomato juice, clam chowder and so on.

A : I'll have the shrimp cocktail. And I'll also have the cream of mushroom soup and the beet and cucumber salad.

W : Very well, sir. What kind of salad dressing would you like, sir? We have French dressing, thousand island, mayonnaise and blue cheese dressing.

A : French dressing please. The steak won't take too long to cook, will it? I'm starved.

W : I bet it will be ready as soon as you finish your appetizer and soup. And what kind of dessert would you like, sir?

A : Vanilla ice-cream, please.

W : Thank you for your order. I get it for you right away, sir.

Conversation 3 What about Your Main Course?

Ⓦ : Waiter Ⓖ : Guest

W : Good evening. May I take your order?

G : Yes, please.

W : What would you like?

G : I'd like to start with the vegetable soup.

W : All right. And what about your main course?

G : Broiled lobster with a salad.

W : Sounds good, sir.

Conversation 4 I'm Going To Repeat Your Order Items.

Ⓜ : Man ⓌⓄ : Woman Ⓦ : Waitress

W : Good afternoon, ma'am, sir. My name's Young. Here are the menus. Would you care for some drinks?

M : Yes, I'll take a dry sherry.

W : And for you, ma'am?

Wo : Well, a glass of water is fine with me.

W : OK. I'll be back with your drinks.

(The waitress comes back with the guests' drinks.)

W : Excuse me. Here's your water, ma'am. Here's your drink, sir. Are you ready to order now?

M : Yes. I'd like the house salad and the sirloin steak.

W : What kind of dressing would you like? We have Thousand Island, French, and Italian.

M : French dressing, please.

W : How would you like your steak, sir?

M : Medium rare, please.

W : Yes, a medium rare sirloin steak. What would you like with that, sir?

M : Baked potato with sour cream, please.

W : Yes, baked potato with sour cream. What would you like to start with, ma'am?

Wo : What's the soup of the day?

W : It's cream of mushroom, ma'am.

Wo : Well, I don't like that. I'll have a shrimp cocktail for the appetizer and one grilled sole for the entrée.

W : A shrimp cocktail and a grilled sole. Any side order, ma'am?

Wo : May I have some garlic bread?

W : Of course, ma'am.

M : Excuse me. May I have some rice?

W : No problem, sir. I'm going to repeat your order items. One house salad with French dressing, one medium-rare sirloin steak, a baked potato with sour cream, and rice, sir. One shrimp cocktail, one grilled sole, and some garlic bread for you, ma'am. Are those correct?

M & Wo : Yes.

W : OK. Anything else?

Wo : Excuse me. Can I have a large coke?

W : Sure. One large coke. Very good! Thank you. Your orders won't take long.

Practice Point

Complete the following conversations relating to the previous Conversations.

1

Waiter : Would you like a baked potato or (   ) fries?
Mrs. Brown : A baked potato with sour cream.

2

Mrs. Brown : What salad (   ) with the steak?
Waiter : You have a choice of either lettuce and tomato or beet and cucumber.

3

Guest : I'd like to start (   ) the vegetable soup.
Waiter : All right. And what about your main courses?

4

Guest : What's the soup of the (   )?
Waiter : It's cream of mushroom, ma'am.

Unit 4

Korean Restaurant

Introduction to the Job Field

Reading 1: Traditional Korean Food

The traditional Korean meal includes rice, soup, and many kinds of side dishes. Boiled rice, called "Bap," is a basic element of Korean cuisine and is served in an individual bowl. Soups are a common part of any Korean meal. Unlike other cultures, in Korean culture, soup is served as part of the main course rather than at the beginning or the end of the meal as an accompaniment to rice along with other side dishes. Side dishes are shared with other family members. An authentic Korean meal often includes a minimum of five different side dishes. Although there are many types of side dishes, the most important and well-known is kimchi.

Reading 2: Procedure for Credit Card Payment

Currently credit cards are used to pay for food and beverages, airline tickets, and other products and service purchases. As an employee of a restaurant, you should know the procedures for accepting credit card payments.

Procedure for Credit Card Payment

All employees should acknowledge the following procedure to give the best service to their guests.

(1) Ensure the validity of the credit card. The expiry date appears on the card. If the card is invalid, you should check it with the appropriate credit card company.

(2) Confirm the signature of the guest on the credit card. If the signature does not appear on the credit card, you should ask the guest to show identification, then sign the card on the spot.

(3) The amount to be paid should not exceed the limit approved by the credit card company. In case of exceeding the amount, authorization should be obtained from the credit card company.

(4) Damaged credit cards are not valid. Also verify that the card is not on the blacklist of the credit card company.

Prep. for Conversation

Vocabulary 1: Vegetables & Fruits

Match each word in the first column with its meaning in the second column.

(1) cucumber •	• ⓐ 양파
(2) Chinese cabbage •	• ⓑ 파
(3) pea •	• ⓒ 깨
(4) sesame •	• ⓓ 고추
(5) green pepper •	• ⓔ 당근
(6) green onion/scallion •	• ⓕ 시금치
(7) carrot •	• ⓖ 양상추
(8) mushroom •	• ⓗ 배추
(9) red pepper •	• ⓘ 건포도
(10) lettuce •	• ⓙ 죽순
(11) bamboo shoot •	• ⓚ 피망, 풋고추
(12) raisin •	• ⓛ 완두콩
(13) spinach •	• ⓜ 버섯
(14) onion •	• ⓝ 오이

Vocabulary 2: How to Cook

Match each word in the first column with its meaning in the second column.

(1) dip	ⓐ 자르다, 썰다
(2) grind	ⓑ 빻다
(3) peel	ⓒ 얇게 베다
(4) slice	ⓓ 껍질을 벗기다
(5) chop	ⓔ 적시다
(6) bake	ⓕ 양념에 담가 절이다
(7) boil	ⓖ 빵, 과자를 오븐에 굽다
(8) smoke	ⓗ 끓이다, 삶다
(9) mince	ⓘ 으깨다
(10) mash	ⓙ 다지다, 잘게 썰다
(11) stew	ⓚ 훈제하다
(12) marinate	ⓛ 은근한 불로 끓이다, 찌다
(13) fry	ⓜ 기름에 튀기다

Key Expressions: Korean Food Service

How can you say the following in English?

1. 불고기는 외국인에게 가장 인기 있는 한국의 요리입니다.

....

(Bulgogi, the most, popular, dishes, Korean, foreigners, among, of, one, is)

2. 무엇이 한국의 전통술인가요?

....

(what's, Korean, traditional, liquor, ?)

3. 어느 것을 선택할지 모르겠습니다.

(which, choose, to, we're not, sure)

4. 한정식은 밥, 국, 많은 반찬이 나옵니다.

(Hanjeongsik, rice, a bowl of, soup, and, many, side dishes, with, consists of)

5. 구운 생선도 나옵니다.

(fish, broiled, also, is, served)

6. 맥주 2병 갖다 주세요.

(beer, two, bottles, bring, of, please)

7. 맛있게 드세요.

(your meal, enjoy, please)

8. 바로 갖다드리겠어요.

(I'll, some, right away, bring)

9. 요리하는 데 시간이 걸립니다.

(It'll, a while, take, to, cook)

10. 기다리겠습니까?

(Would, mind, you, waiting, please, ?)

Practice Makes Perfect

Conversation 1 Recommending Particular Korean Dishes

Ⓦ : Waiter Ⓖ : Guest

W : Good evening, sir. Would you care to order your dinner?

G : I don't know anything about Korean food. Could you recommend something for me?

W : Yes. Bulgogi is one of the most popular Korean dishes among foreigners in our restaurant.

G : What is it?

W : It's sliced beef that you roast on a charcoal burner right at your table. Bulgogi consists of strips of beef charcoal-roasted over a brazier at the table after it has been marinated in a complex mixture of soy sauce, sesame oil and spices for a few hours. We usually have it with rice and wrap it in raw lettuce.

G : Okay. I've never tried Bulgogi, but I'll have it this time.

W : Would you like something to drink, sir? We have beer, wine and traditional Korean liquor.

G : What's traditional Korean liquor?

W : It's called 'Soju'. It's one of the most popular drinks among Korean people. I think 'Soju' goes very well with this.

G : Good. I'll try it. Bring a bottle of Soju, please.

W : Thank you so much.

Conversation 2 Taking an Order for Hanjeongsik

Ⓦ : Waitress Ⓖ : Guest

W : Good afternoon, sir. May I take your order?

G : We're not sure which to choose, but we'd like to have traditional Korean food. Would you help us to choose a Korean dish?

W : Certainly, sir. I'd like to suggest Hanjeongsik. Hanjeongsik is one of many typical Korean style dishes. It consists of a bowl of rice and soup with many side dishes. The side dishes consist of bean sprouts, kimchi, an assortment of broiled seafood, stewed beef ribs, deep fried shrimp and vegetables. And a fried or broiled fish is also served. I think you have a good opportunity to try this typical Korean food.

G : All right. We'll take it.

W : Do you wish anything to drink, sir?

G : Yes. We'd like beer. Bring two bottles, please.

(Later)

W : Enjoy your meal, please.

G : Waitress! We need some salt. There's none on the table.

W : Yes. I'll bring some right away.

Conversation 3 Taking an order for Broiled Beef

Ⓦ : Waiter Ⓖ : Guest

W : How are you doing, sir?

G : Fine, thank you.

W : Are you waiting for somebody, sir?

G : No, we're all here.

W : Oh, I see. Here's the menu, sir.

(Later)

What do you want to order for dinner?

G : I really don't know about Korean food. Can you suggest a Korean dish?

W : Yes. I can recommend broiled beef ribs table d'hote.

G : What is it?

W : It consists of broiled beef ribs, assorted fresh vegetables, seasonal wild greens and spinach, pan-fried fish and vegetables with egg, rice soup, and fresh fruits in season.

G : Is it spicy?

W : No, it isn't.

G : That sounds good. We'll try that.

W : That'll take a while to cook. Would you mind waiting, please?

G : That's okay.

W : Thanks a lot. We'll try to prepare your order as soon as possible.

Conversation 4 Recommending the Best Food

Ⓦ : Waiter Ⓑ : Mr. Brown Ⓒ : Mr. Clington

W : Good afternoon, gentlemen. Are you ready to order now?

B : Well, can you recommend the best food in this restaurant?

W : Yes. May I suggest the Korean traditional food, bulgogi, sir? Many foreigners like it.

C : What is bulgogi?

W : It's minced beef which has been marinated in a mixed sauce containing salt, sesame oil and garlic for a few hours and then is cooked over an open charcoal flame at your table. It is something like American barbecue, sir.

B : Is it hot? I heard every dish is hot in Korea.

W : No, sir. It's very mild. It's served with rice and various kinds of kimchi. Some kinds of kimchi are pretty spicy, and others are something like German sauerkraut.

C : O.K. Please bring us two portions of bulgogi.

W : What would you like to drink, gentlemen?
Beer goes well with this.

B : Fine, bring us two beers.

W : Very well, gentlemen.

Conversation 5 Paying in Cash

Ⓒ : Cashier Ⓖ : Guest

C : Did you enjoy your meal, sir?

G : Very good. I'll pay my bill now. How much is it?

C : Wait a minute, please. It'll be 97,000 won altogether, sir.

G : What's this total for?

C : Your bill includes a 10% tax and a 10% service charge.

G : I see.

C : How would you like to pay, sir?

G : In cash, please.

C : Thank you, sir. You gave me 100,000 won. Your change is 3,000 won and here is your receipt.

G : You can keep the change.

C : I'm sorry, sir. Our policy is no tipping. Have a nice day.

Conversation 6 Paying by Credit Card

C : Cashier G : Guest

C : How was your lunch, ma'am?

G : It was very delicious. I'd like to pay my bill.

C : The charge for your lunch is 30 dollars, ma'am.

G : Can I use my credit card?

C : Yes, ma'am. What do you have?

G : Visa.

C : Okay. May I have your card, please?

G : Here it is.

C : Could you sign here, ma'am?

G : All right. Here you are.

C : Here's your receipt and card, ma'am.

G : Thank you.

C : I hope we'll serve you again soon.

Conversation 7 Paying by Traveler's Check

C : Cashier G : Guest

C : Good evening, sir. I hope you enjoyed your stay with us.

G : Oh, yes. We did very much. I want to settle my bill.

C : The full amount is 108,000 won including tax and service charge.

G : I'll pay by traveler's checks. Do you accept traveler's checks here?

C : Certainly, sir. The total will be ninety-six dollars.

G : Here's a one hundred dollar traveler's check.

C : May I see your passport, sir?

G : Here you are. What's the rate of exchange today?

C : It's 1,120 won per dollar today. Sign here with this pen, please.

G : Sure. Here it is.

C : Thank you very much. Here's your change and your passport.
See you again, sir.

Conversation 8 Adding the Breakfast Bill to the Room Account

C : Cashier G : Guest

C : Good morning, sir. How was your breakfast?

G : I enjoyed my breakfast very much.

C : Thanks, sir.

G : I want to pay my bill.

C : Your bill comes to 30,000 won, sir.

G : I'd like to charge it to my room account.

C : What room are you in?

G : My room is 903. I'll stay there till tomorrow.

C : Wait a minute, sir. Your name is Frank Lewis. Is that right?

G : Sure. That's right.

C : Could you please sign here, sir?

G : Yes, here you are.

C : Thank you, sir.

Conversation 9 Dealing with a Miscalculation

C : Cashier G : Guest

G : Excuse me. There's something wrong on my bill.

C : What's it, sir?

G : I'm afraid you've overcharged me. You've charged me for two cocktails, but I only had one. And I never had another side dish. Look at this. You made this bill wrong.

C : Oh, is that so? I think we made a mistake on your bill. I'll check it with bartender right away.

(After a while)

I'm really sorry, sir. You're right. I'll adjust your bill immediately, sir.

G : That's okay.

C : I look forward to serving you again, sir.

Practice Point

Complete the following conversations relating to the previous Conversations.

1

Guest : Good. I'll try it. Bring a (   ) of Soju, please.

Waiter : Thank you so much.

2

Waiter : Good afternoon, sir. May I (   ) your order?

Guest : We're not sure which to choose.

3

Waiter : Are you (   ) for somebody, sir?

Guest : No, we're all here.

4

Mr. Brown : Is it hot? I heard every dish is hot in Korea.

Waiter : No, sir. It's very (   ).

5

Cashier : Your change is 3,000 won, and here is your receipt.

Guest : You can ( ) the change.

6

Guest : Can I use my ( ) card?

Cashier : Yes, ma'am. What do you have?

7

Guest : Here you are. What's the ( ) of exchange today?

Cashier : It's 1,120 won per dollar today. Sign here with this pen.

8

Cashier : Your bill comes to 30,000 won, sir.

Guest : I'd like to ( ) it to my room account.

9

Guest : I'm afraid you've overcharged me. You've charged me for two cocktails, but I only had one. And I never had another side dish. Look at this. You made this bill ( ).

Cashier : Oh, is that so? I think we made a mistake on your bill.

Unit 5

Banquet Service

Introduction to the Job Field

Reading 1: Banquet

A banquet is a large meal or feast, complete with main courses and desserts. It usually serves a purpose, such as a charitable gathering, a ceremony, or a celebration, often preceded or followed by speeches in honor of someone. Banquets have been used as a formal occasion for thousands of years. Royalty and higher classes have frequently thrown banquets for special events, such as birthdays, weddings, and holidays. Some banquets are used to signing a treaty or agreements of some sort. Business banquets are a popular way to strengthen bonds between businessmen and their partners. It is common that a banquet is organized at the end of an academic conference.

The banquet manager effectively and proactively monitors the daily functions of the Banquet Department. This includes providing support and guidance to the banquet team, the Catering and Convention Services team, and Banquet Beverage. This also includes working and communicating closely with all hotel departments. Banquet Managers are an integral part of the hotel's overall Food and Beverage team. The colleagues will work along with the Restaurant Manager, Beverage Manager, and Room Service Manager to ensure a successful Food & Beverage Team.

Reading 2: Western Style Table Manner

(1) You should wait at the entrance of the restaurant until the waiter or waitress comes to guide you to your seat. Do not go straight to the table by yourself. In case of a fast food restaurant, you may go straight to any seat.

(2) When you're sitting at a table, sit up straight and comfortable. Do not rest your elbows on the table.

(3) Do not tuck in or tie your napkin around your neck. The napkin belongs on your lap.

(4) Use the outside fork and knife first. The Europeans hold the knife in their right hand, and the fork in their left, while the Americans change the fork from the left to their right hand after cutting their food. Never eat with your knife.

(5) Eat soup as quickly as possible, with no sucking noises; this applies to coffee or tea, too.

(6) You can have a conversation. However, do not speak with your mouth full.

(7) In case you have to leave the table during our meal, put your napkin on the armrest or on the back of the chair. Otherwise, the waiter or waitress will take your dish away.

Reading 3: Main dish & Desserts

A main course is the featured or primary dish in a meal consisting of several courses. It usually follows the entrée ("entry") course, and the salad course. In North American usage it may in fact be called the "entrée".

The main course is usually the heaviest, heartiest, and most complex or substantive dish on a menu. The main ingredient is usually meat or fish; in vegetarian meals, the main course sometimes attempts to mimic a meat course. It is most often preceded by an appetizer, soup, or salad, and followed by a dessert. For those reasons the main course is sometimes referred to as the "meat course".

In formal dining, a well-planned main course can function as a sort of gastronomic apex or climax. In such a scheme, the preceding courses are designed to prepare for and lead up to the main course in such a way that the main course is anticipated and, when the scheme is successful, increased in its ability to satisfy and delight the diner.

In Western culture dessert is a course that typically comes at the end of a meal, usually consisting of sweet food. Common desserts include cakes, cookies, pastries, ice cream, pie, and candies. Fruit may also be eaten with the dessert. In Russia, breakfast foods such as Bliny, Oladi, and Syrniki served with honey and jam are also popular as desserts.

Prep. for Conversation

Vocabulary 1: Spices / Condiments

Match each word in the first column with its meaning in the second column.

(1) salt •	• ⓐ 설탕
(2) mustard •	• ⓑ 생강
(3) ginger •	• ⓒ 겨자
(4) sugar •	• ⓓ 마늘
(5) vinegar •	• ⓔ 간장
(6) pepper •	• ⓕ 소금
(7) garlic •	• ⓖ 참기름
(8) sesame oil •	• ⓗ 식초
(9) soybean sauce •	• ⓘ 후추

Vocabulary 2: Meat

Match each word in the first column with its meaning in the second column.

(10) beef •	• ⓙ 돼지고기
(11) pork •	• ⓚ 닭고기
(12) chicken •	• ⓛ 소고기
(13) duck •	• ⓜ 송아지고기
(14) veal •	• ⓝ 오리고기
(15) mutton(lamb) •	• ⓞ 칠면조고기
(16) turkey •	• ⓟ 양고기

Key Expressions: Banquet Service

How can you say the following in English?

1. 연단과 연설자를 위한 마이크를 설치합시다.

(a podium, a microphone, and, speakers, for, get, let's)

2. 전등과 에어컨이 잘 가동되고 있습니까?

(the lighting, air-conditioning, and, properly, working, is, ?)

3. 다음 식사 코스는 무엇입니까?

(follow, to, what, ?)

4. 연어 대신 닭고기 종류로 대체할 수 있습니까?

(some kind of chicken, the salmon, for, I, can, substitute, ?)

5. 연어 대신 코니쉬 닭으로 대체해 드릴 수 있습니다.

(We'll, substitute, the cornish hen, be able to, the salmon, for)

6. 흔히 마시는 음료는 준비될 수 있겠지요?

(the usual drinks, arranged, be, can, ?)

7. 그렇게 하면 작은 바를 설치할 수 있는 공간이 충분히 나옵니다.

(that, plenty of space, would, a little bar, leave, for, to be set up)

8. 당신이 음료를 준비해 주십시오.

....

(I'd like, to arrange, you, the drinks)

9. 제 비서에게 견적서를 보내 주십시오.

....

(you, an estimate, send, my secretary, could, to)

10. 음식값(봉사료, 세금 등)은 1인당 25프랑 되겠습니다.

....

(the menu cost, 25 francs, would, head, per, be, about)

Practice Makes Perfect

Conversation 1 Reserving a Banquet Room

Ⓜ : Manager Ⓖ : Guest

M : Good afternoon. Banquet Manager. May I help you?

G : Yes, please. This is Mr. Kim, Samsung company. We'll have a reception for a dinner we're planning. Could you provide me with some information about your facilities for reception?

M : Yes, when is the reception planned for, Mr. Kim?

G : October 15th.

M : For what time would that be, Mr. Kim?

G : 6:00 p.m.

M : How many people will be coming, Mr. Kim?

G : We're planning to have a reception for about 50 people.

M : We have two suitable banquet rooms to use for 50 people on that date and hour. What sort of service would you like, Mr. Kim?

G : It'll be a dinner party for our personnel.

M : How much per person do you expect to spend?

G : We're planning about 40,000 won.

M : What kind of food would you like to have, Mr. Kim?

G : We'll have steak. Will you fax us an estimate right away for this reception including the food and beverages to be served?

M : Yes, I'll do so. What's your fax number and telephone number, Mr. Kim?

G : My fax number is 792-1123 and my telephone number is 792-1124.

M : Thank you. I'll send it right away.

Conversation 2 Pre-checking the Banquet Room

Ⓜ : Manager Ⓖ : Guest

M : Good morning, sir. This is the banquet manager, Mrs. Kim. May I help you?

G : I'd like to make a reservation for our seminar on October 15th, at 6 o'clock. Can I see a banquet room today?

M : Yes. What time will you get here, sir?

G : Maybe I'll get there at 4:30 p.m. Is that all right?

M : Certainly, sir. We'll wait for you. How many people would there be, sir?

G : Maybe there'll be about 300 people. We'll hold the seminar for some invited professors.

(Later)

I called your office this morning. I'd like to see the banquet room first.

M : Yes, sir. It's on the third floor. This way, please.

G : Oh, it looks good for our seminar. We'd like to have dinner at that time. Will you make up an estimate for our seminar?

M : Yes, sir. I'll call you at your office when I am ready for you. And if you decide to hold your seminar at our hotel, please let me know.

G : Sure. Thank you very much.

Conversation 3 Cancelling a Reservation of Facilities

C : Clerk G : Guest

C : Good afternoon. Can I help you?

G : Yes, I'd like to speak to the manager.

C : I'm sorry, sir. He isn't in the office. May I take a message?

G : Yes. I reserved a function room for a family party tomorrow evening, but I'll have to cancel it.

C : May I ask your name, please?

G : Frank Lewis.

C : Okay, Mr. Lewis. I'll make sure the manager will get the message. Thank you for calling, Mr. Lewis.

Conversation 4 Holding an International Conference

C : Clerk G : Guest

C : Good morning, Catering Office, may I help you?

G : Yes, please. My name is John Brown, B-R-O-W-N, calling from the States. An international conference will take place at your hotel on July the 25th through 27th, this year 2006. Are you familiar with our conference?

C : Certainly, Mr. Brown. Isn't that the American Chamber of Commerce, the AMCHAM Conference?

G : Exactly. I am the Executive Director of ABE, the American Beef Exporting Company, and I am representing the company.

C : Very good, Mr. Brown. But the organizer of the conference has already booked the plenary meeting room and a couple of dining rooms.

G : Great. Our company has invited a group of 30 people. Our company's staff will be 5 and the others are our guests.

C : How many rooms and what type of room would you like, Mr. Brown?

G : We will need a meeting room for 30 people, furnished with meeting tables, an over-head projector with a screen, a couple of microphones and a lectern, please.

C : How long or how many hours would you need?

G : I really don't know exactly, but definitely more than 4 hours daily. With reference to the time schedule concerning the conference, the plenary meeting will take an hour starting at 9 o'clock in the morning each day. After the plenary meeting, all the invited groups will have individual workshops. Those individual workshops will take about 4 hours a day, 2 hours in the morning and 2 hours in the afternoon.

C : Would you need anything else, Mr. Brown? For instance, writing pads, mineral water, coffee, tea or any snacks during workshops?

G : Thank you for your advice, but on the last day, our workshop won't take longer than an hour. Will there be any special charges for that?

C : Don't worry, Mr. Brown. That will be complimentary. But the meeting supplies and beverages will be charged on a consumption basis. The use of furniture and equipment will also be complimentary.

G : Great. Will you send us the contract listing all those points?

C : Yes, Mr. Brown. You will receive two copies of the contract. One copy is to be kept for you and the other to be returned to us. Please sign and return the original and retain the other copy for your own use.

Practice Point

Complete the following conversations relating to the previous Conversations.

1

Manager : How (   ) people will be coming, Mr. Kim?

Guest : We're planning to have a reception for about 50 people.

2

Manager : I'll call you at your office when I am ready for you. And if you decide to hold your seminar at our hotel, please let me (   ).

Guest : Sure. Thank you very much.

3

Guest : I'm sorry, sir. He isn't in the office. May I (   ) a message?

Clerk : Yes. I reserved a function room for a family party tomorrow evening, but I'll have to cancel it.

4

Clerk : How many rooms and what type of room would you like, Mr. Brown?

Guest : We will need a meeting room for 30 people, (   ) with meeting tables, an over-head projector with a screen, a couple of microphones and a lectern, please.

Unit 6

Coffee Shop & Bar Services

Introduction to the Job Field

Reading 1: Beverage Serving Manners

- Drinks are usually carried on a tray in a restaurant. Therefore, tray carrying skills are important for any restaurant employee.
- Trays are usually carried on the palm of the hand with the tips of the fingers slightly raised: Do not hold the tray by its edges.
- Drink trays are usually held in the left hand, so that the right hand is free to serve the drinks.
- Service staff should handle glassware by the base or the stem: Never handle glasses by their rims, never put fingers in the glasses.
- Trays should be carried at waist level, walking with a straight back and shoulders.
- All drinks should be announced when being placed on the table: This provides an element of customer service as well as providing the guest with an opportunity to check that they are being served the drink they ordered.

Reading 2: Bartender

A bartender or cocktail waitress should be familiar with the English names of all sorts of liquors and mixed drinks. Especially, the bartender must know how to make various kinds of beverages for the guests. The bartender also supervises his waiters or waitresses. He must handle various kinds of reports, such as stock control, inventory, daily sales reports, and so on. The bartender's polite and witty conversation with the guests can create a most pleasant atmosphere in the bar.

Prep. for Conversation

Vocabulary: Drinks

Match each word in the first column with its meaning in the second column.

(1) decaffeinated coffee	•	•	ⓐ 고급 포도주
(2) coke	•	•	ⓑ 라거맥주
(3) lager beer	•	•	ⓒ 생맥주
(4) black coffee	•	•	ⓓ 콜라
(5) draft beer	•	•	ⓔ 크림과 설탕을 넣지 않은 커피
(6) mineral water	•	•	ⓕ 생수
(7) vintage wine	•	•	ⓖ 사과 주스(탄산음료)
(8) cider	•	•	ⓗ 카페인이 없는 커피

Key Expressions: Coffee Shop & Bar Service

How can you say the following in English?

1. 커피는 어떻게 해드릴까요?

....

(your coffee, how, like, would, you, please?)

2. 커피 더 드릴까요?

....

(some more, you, would, coffee, like, ?)

3. 베이컨을 아주 바삭바삭하게 요리해 주세요.

....

(bacon, crisp, please, have, cooked, very)

4. 음료하시겠어요?

....

(you, something, care, to drink, for, would, ?)

5. 물이면 됩니다.

....

(Water, fine, be, will)

6. 이것은 제가 주문한 게 아닌데요.

....

(this, I, what, ordered, not, is)

7. 병맥주가 아니라 생맥주를 주문했습니다.

....

(I, for, draught beer, bottled beer, asked, not)

8. 한 잔 더 시키지 않았는데요.

....

(I, didn't, another, order, drink)

9. 이것은 술집에서 내는 겁니다.

....

(this, the house, is, on)

10. 10% 봉사료가 포함되어 있습니다.

....

(a 10% service charge, included, is)

Practice Makes Perfect

Conversation 1 an Order for Coffee

W : Waiter G : Guest

W : Good afternoon, ma'am. How are you?

G : Fine, thank you.

W : May I take your order, ma'am?

G : Not yet. Please give me a few more minutes.

W : Please take your time, ma'am.

(Later)

Are you ready to order now, ma'am?

G : Yes, please.

W : What would you like to have, ma'am?

G : Regular coffee, please. Make it real hot.

W : Thank you, ma'am.

(Later)

Would you like some more coffee, ma'am?

G : No, thanks. I've had enough.

Conversation 2 an Order for Breakfast

Ⓦ : Waiter Ⓖ : Guest

W : Good morning, sir. Here's the menu. What would you like to order for breakfast?

G : I'll have hash brown potatoes, a corn muffin, ham and eggs.

W : How would you like your eggs, sir?

G : Turned over, please.

W : What would you care to drink, sir?

G : Coffee, please.

W : How would you like your coffee, please?

G : Regular coffee, please.

W : Is there anything else, sir?

G : No. That's all.

W : Thank you for your order, sir.

(Later)

Would you like a refill on your coffee?

G : Yes, just a little more, please.

Conversation 3 an Order for an American Breakfast

Ⓦ : Waiter Ⓖ : Guest

W : Good morning, sir. Can I have your order?

G : Yes, I'd like to order an American breakfast.

W : What kind of juice would you like, sir?

G : Tomato juice, please.

W : How would you like your eggs, sir?

G : A fried egg, sunny-side-up.

W : Would you like bacon, sausage or ham, sir?

G : I'll take bacon. Have it cooked very crisp, please.

W : Yes, sir. Would you like anything else, sir?

G : Coffee, please.

W : Thank you, sir.

Conversation 4 an Order for a Continental Breakfast

Ⓦ : Waiter Ⓖ : Guest

W : Good morning, ma'am. Are you ready to order?

G : Yes. I'd like a continental breakfast.

W : What kind of fruit juice will you have, ma'am?

G : Tomato juice, please.

W : We have some bread and cornflakes, or oatmeal, ma'am.

G : I'll have cornflakes with milk and corn muffins with marmalade.

W : All right, ma'am. Coming right up.

Conversation 5 Orders for Lunch

Ⓦ : Waitress Ⓖ : Guest

W : Good afternoon, sir. What would you like to have?

G1 : Well. Beef steak and French fries, please.

W : How would you like your steak, sir?

G1 : I'd like it medium, please.

W : What kind of dressings would you like, sir?

G1 : I'd like Italian on my salad.

W : Would you care for something to drink, sir?

G1 : I want some coffee, please.

W : What would you like, sir?

G2 : Hamburger steak, orange juice and some coffee, please.

W : Anything else, sir?

G1 : That's okay.

W : Thank you so much. I'll be right with you.

(Later)

G1 : Waitress! I asked for this to be a medium steak. It's rare.

W : I'm very sorry. I'll take it back and have it cooked some more.

G1 : Thanks.

Conversation 6 Orders for Dinner

W : Waiter G : Guest

W : Good evening, sir. May I take your order?

G1 : What would you recommend from today's special menu?

W : Today's special is filet mignon, sir. It's very tasty.

G1 : Well, we'll order two filet mignons.

W : How do you want your steak, sir?

G1 : One medium.

G2 : Well done, please.

W : What would you like as soups, sir?

G1 : Vegetable soup, please.

W : What kind of salad dressing would you like, sir?

G1 : Thousand Island, please.

G2 : French dressing.

W : Would you care for some wine, sir?

G1 : Yes, I'd like a red wine with my meal.

G2 : Me, too.

W : Could I serve you anything else, sir?

G1 : Yes, water will be fine.

(Later)

W : What do you want for dessert, sir?

G1 : I'd like strawberry ice cream.

G2 : Coffee, please.

W : We hope you enjoyed your dinner.

G1 : That meal was delicious.

W : I'm glad you liked it.

Conversation 7 Orders for a Whisky

Ⓦ : Waiter Ⓖ : Guest

W : Good evening, sir. What can I get you?

G1 : I'd like to have a Scotch and Soda.

W : What brand of Scotch would you like, sir?

G1 : Johnnie Walker Red, please.

W : What would you like to drink, sir?

G2 : I'll have a glass of whisky.

W : What kind of whisky do you want, sir? We have Scotch, Irish, American, and Canadian whisky.

G2 : I'll have an American whisky.

W : How would you care for your whisky, sir?

G2 : On the rocks, please.

W : Thank you, sir.

Conversation 8 Orders for Brandy & Gin

Ⓦ : Waiter Ⓖ : Guest

W : Good evening, gentlemen. May I help you?

G1 : Yes, I want to drink a Cognac.

W : Which brand would you prefer, sir?

G1 : Well. A shot of Remy Martin X.O. No ice, no water, please.

W : And you, sir?

G2 : Give me a Gilbey's, please.

W : Would you like it straight up or on the rocks?

G2 : Straight up, please. And could you give us some dry snacks?

W : Yes, sir. Thank you very much.

Conversation 9 Orders for Liquor & Beer

Ⓦ : Waiter Ⓖ : Guest

W : Good evening, ladies and gentlemen.

G1 : We need a table for four. Do you have a table by the window?

W : Yes. Please step this way. Here's your seat. How is it?

G2 : Oh, it'll do fine.

W : What may I offer you, ladies and gentlemen?

G1 : We don't know what we want. Wait a moment. please.

(Later)

I'd like a glass of Drambuie.

G2 : A glass of Bailey's Irish cream, please.

G3 : Cointreau, please.

W : What would you like, sir?

G4 : A bottle of beer for me.

W : Do you want any special brand, sir?

G4 : No. Anything will be fine. I'm very thirsty.

W : And what kind of side dishes would you like?

G1 : Bring us some peanuts, please.

W : Yes, I'll bring them right away.

(Later)

Here they are. Taste these liquors, please. Would these be all right?

G1 : Yes. Very good.

G2 : Good.

G3 : Yes. That's okay.

W : Thank you very much.

Conversation 10 Orders for a Cocktail

Ⓦ : Waiter Ⓖ : Guest

W : Good evening, gentlemen.

G1 : A table for three by the window?

W : Certainly, sir. This way, please. Will this table be all right, gentlemen?

G2 : Oh, yes. It's wonderful.

W : What will you have, sir?

G1 : I'll have a Martini.

W : How would you like it, sir?

G1 : Don't make it strong, please.

G2 : A Singapore Sling, please. And make it with a lot of soda water, please.

W : And you, sir?

G3 : I'm driving. I want a cocktail without alcohol.

W : We have Pussy Foot, Fruit Punch, Virgin Mary, Shirley Temple, Virgin Pina Colada, and Lemonade.

G3 : Pussy Foot, please.

Conversation 11 Orders for Wine

Ⓦ : Waiter Ⓖ : Guest

W : Good evening, sir. What would you like to drink?

G1 : I'd like to have a French red wine.

W : What brand would you prefer, sir?

G1 : Well. I'd like a bottle of Chateau Margaux, Margaux 1988 (Red Bordeaux). This wine is my favorite one.

W : Which would you like better, dry or sweet wine?

G1 : Dry wine, please.

W : What would you have, ma'am?

G2 : Can you recommend a white wine?

W : Yes. I'd like to recommend the Chablis, ma'am. This is a mild wine.

And it's very popular with our foreign guests.

G2 : Okay. I'll try that one.

W : Thank you, ma'am. Do you need anything else?

G2 : Would you bring us some cheese, please?

W : Certainly, ma'am.

Practice Point

Complete the following conversations relating to the previous Conversations.

1

Guest : Not yet. Please give me a few more minutes.
Waiter : Please (   ) your time, ma'am.

2

Waiter : How would you like your eggs, sir?
Guest : Turned (   ), please.

3

Waiter : Would you like bacon, sausage or ham, sir?
Guest : I'll take bacon. Have it (   ) very crisp, please.

4

Waiter : What kind of (   ) juice will you have, ma'am?
Guest : Tomato juice, please.

5

Waiter : What kind of (   ) would you like, sir?

Guest : I'd like Italian on my salad.

6

Waiter : Good evening, sir. May I take your order?

Guest : What would you (   ) from today's special menu?

7

Waiter : What (   ) of Scotch would you like, sir?

Guest : Johnnie Walker Red, please.

8

Waiter : Would you like it straight up or (   ) the rocks?

Guest : Straight up, please.

9

Waiter : And what kind of (   ) dishes would you like?

Guest : Bring us some peanuts, please.

10

Waiter : (   ) would you like it, sir?

Guest : Don't make it strong, please.

11

Waiter : Which would you like better, dry or (   ) wine?

Guest : Dry wine, please.

CHAPTER 2

ROOM & OTHER SERVICES

Unit 1

Reservations & Telephone Services

Introduction to the Job Field

Reading 1: Room Reservations

Room reservations come in by letter, telephone, and internet. If a hotel is able to accept a booking, the reservations clerk must record it. The reservations clerk normally completes a reservation form and enters the information in a diary. These days reservations are usually organized with a computer, but some hotels may still use room charts to record the information. Files are organized by date and within each date, names are listed alphabetically. Filing the information makes it easier for the hotel to locate the records when the customer arrives.

The reservations department keeps records of how the guest is arriving, at what time, and for how long. This information, including the type of facilities wanted, must be communicated to the room clerk. Keeping track of the number of rooms reserved and the number available is the biggest responsibility of the reservation department.

After the reservation is made, it is usually confirmed via phone, e-mail, fax, or letter and most often includes a reservation number.

Reading 2: Telephone Operator

The telephone operators work at the switchboard in the hotel around the clock and every outside call to the hotel must be answered by them. The telephone operators work behind the scene of the front desk. They are considered front-desk employees, and like the rest they must be able to give information about the services of the hotel. To help people calling the hotel from outside, they keep a record of current room assignments. They also take messages in the event that a guest cannot be located.

One of the unique services in most hotels that is still taken care of by the switchboard is the wake-up call. This kind of call wakes up the guest at a prespecified time. Telephone service provides a small source of revenue for most hotels, since a charge is made for outgoing calls in most places. A record of these charges is forwarded to the accounting office as quickly as possible. Outgoing local and long-distance calls are handled by automatic, direct-dial equipment. Calls between guest rooms or from guests to departments such as room service no longer require an operator.

Telephone operators must be courteous, helpful, correct and prompt in their service to the guests.

Prep. for Conversation

Vocabulary 1: Types of Guest Rooms

Match each word in the first column with its meaning in the second column.

(1) single room •	• ⓐ 3인용 객실
(2) double room •	• ⓑ 1인용 침대 2개가 있는 객실
(3) twin room •	• ⓒ 2인용 침대 1개가 있는 객실
(4) triple room •	• ⓓ 1인용 침대 1개가 있는 객실
(5) suite •	• ⓔ 응접실이 딸린 객실
(6) executive floor •	• ⓕ 비즈니스 업무 고객들을 위한 객실이 있는 층
(7) studio •	• ⓖ 객실과 객실이 인접해 있는 객실, 객실 사이에 문이 없음
(8) adjoining room •	• ⓗ 객실과 객실이 인접해 있는 객실, 객실 사이에 문이 있음
(9) connecting room •	• ⓘ 주간에 소파로 이용 가능한 침대가 있는 객실

Vocabulary 2: Types of Call

Match each word in the first column with its meaning in the second column.

(1) collect call	•	• ⓐ 시외전화
(2) overseas call	•	• ⓑ 수신자부담전화
(3) long distance call	•	• ⓒ 국제전화
(4) person to person call	•	• ⓓ 대국전화(전화 받는 상대방 누구와도 연결되는 경우에 요금이 부과되는 전화)
(5) station to station call	•	• ⓔ 지명통화(지정인이 없을 때는 전화요금을 지불하지 않는 전화)

Key Expressions: Room Reservations & Telephone

How can you say the following in English?

1. 언제로 예약을 원하십니까?

....

(When, your reservation, to make, would, you, like, sir?)

2. 며칠 간 묵으시겠습니까?

....

(how long, stay, you, would, like, to, ?)

3. 어떤 방을 원하십니까?

....

(what, type, would, like, you, room, of, ?)

4. 죄송하지만 빈방이 없습니다.

(I'm afraid, vacancy, there's, no)

5. 전망 좋은 방 부탁합니다.

(I'd like, a room, a nice view, with)

6. 하루 숙박료는 얼마입니까?

(what, the, rate, daily, is, ?)

7. 죄송하지만 존슨 씨는 통화 중입니다.

(Sorry, Mr. Johnson, the line, on, is, but)

8. 그에게 다시 전화를 걸라고 할까요?

(have, him, call, back, you, I, shall, ?)

9. 그런 성함을 가진 분은 여기에 한 분도 안 계십니다.

(no one, is, there, here, that, by name)

10. 끊지 말고 기다려 주시겠어요?

(you, the line, hold, please, would, ?)

Practice Makes Perfect

Conversation 1 When Accepting a Reservation

Ⓡ : Reservation Clerk Ⓖ : Guest

R : Hotel Shilla Reservations, may I help you?

G : Yes, I'd like to book a room please.

R : When for, sir?

G : May 17th.

R : How long are you going to stay?

G : A couple of nights.

R : What kind of room do you have in mind, sir?

G : A double room with a fine view.
Could you tell me what the rate is?

R : Yes, sir.
One hundred dollars a night including tax and service charge.

G : All right.
I'll take it.

R : May I have your name, please?

G : Robert Brown. B-R-O-W-N.

R : Mr. Robert Brown, a double room with a fine view for the 17th and the 18th of May.

G : That's right.

Thanks, bye now.

R : Good bye, sir.

Conversation 2 When a Room Is Not Available

R : Reservation Clerk G : Guest

R : Reservations, Miss Kim speaking.

Can I help you?

G : Yes, I'd like to make a reservation.

Do you have a single room available from the 8th of July through the 10th?

R : Let me check.

Wait a moment, please. I'm very sorry, sir, we don't have any single rooms left for those dates.

G : How about a double room?

R : No doubles, either.

We have a full house during that period.

G : You have a full house?

R : Yes, sir.

We are fully booked.

G : I'm in trouble.

I should have booked earlier.

R : If you'd like, we can put you on our waiting list.

G : That sounds good. Thank you.

R : I'll contact you as soon as a room is available. Thank you for calling.

Conversation 3 When Changing Reservations

Ⓞ : Operator Ⓡ : Reservation Clerk Ⓖ : Guest

O : Marriot Hotel, may I help you?

G : Yes, please give me the reservation desk.

O : One moment, please.
I'll connect you with the reservation desk.

R : Good morning, reservation desk. May I help you?

G : Good morning. This is Young Kim from the Orient Travel Agency.
I made reservations for Miss Youngsuk Chang and Miss Min Kim.
I'd like some changes on those reservations.

R : Yes, Mr. Kim. Please hold on a minute. I'll check.
We have reservations for Miss Youngsuk Chang on May 11th and Miss Min Kim on May 27th.

G : That's correct.
Please change the reservation for Miss Chang to May 7th and cancel the reservation for Miss Kim.

R : Yes, I understand. I'll change Miss Chang's reservation to 7th of May and cancel Miss Kim's reservation. Please remember your cancellation code number. It is 73125. May I confirm the spelling of your name, Mr. Kim? Y-O-U-N-G-K-I-M. Is that right?

G : Yes, that's correct.

R : May I have your phone number, Mr. Kim?

G : Sure. My phone number is 02-559-7611 in Korea.

R : Thank you, Mr. Kim.

Conversation 4 When Confirming Reservation

R : Reservation Clerk G : Guest

R : Reservations, Miss Lee speaking. May I help you?

G : Yes, I'd like to confirm my reservation.

R : Would you please tell me the date of your reservation?

G : It was for August 15th.

R : May I ask your name please?

G : Tom Smith.

R : Please hold the line, sir. I'll check on that ....
I'm sorry to have kept you waiting, Mr. Smith.
Your room is confirmed from August 15th to 16th.

G : Oh, thank you. See you then, bye.

R : Thanks for calling, sir. Good bye.

Conversation 5 No Reply from the Room

O : Operator G : Guest

O : Inter-Continental Hotel.
May I help you?

G : Yes. Could you put me through to Room 3210?

O : Certainly, sir. Just a moment, please.
The line's busy. Would you like to hold or call back?

G : I'll hold.

O : Thank you for waiting. I'm afraid there is still no reply.
Would you like to leave a message?

G : Yes, I'll do that.

O : I'll connect you with the concierge.

You can leave the message with her.

Conversation 6 Making a Collect Call

O : Operator G : Guest

O : Operator.

G : I'd like to make a collect call to the U.S.

O : Do you know the area code?

G : No, I don't.

O : Which city, please?

G : Atlanta.

O : That's 508.

What number do you want to call?

G : 412-562.

O : And your name, please?

G : Mr. Kim Gilsu.

O : I'll call you back.

It'll take a few minutes, because I have to place the call with the international operator.

G : Okay. Thank you.

Conversation 7 Wake-up Call

Ⓞ : Operator Ⓖ : Guest

G : Could you wake me up at 4:00, please?

O : Yes, sir. What's your room number?

G : 5410.

O : Thank you.

Conversation 8 When the Party Is Not Available

Ⓞ : Operator Ⓖ : Guest

O : Lotte Hotel. May I help you?

G : Yeah, I'd like to speak to Mr. John Anderson in room 1254.

O : Just a moment, ma'am. ....

Hello? I'm sorry, ma'am, but he doesn't reply.

Would you like to leave a message?

G : When he returns, could you have him call me?

O : Certainly, sir.

May I have your name and telephone number?

G : My name is Jannet Jackson and the phone number is 520-4525.

Practice Point

Complete the following conversations relating to the previous Conversations.

1

Reservation Clerk : What kind of room do you have in mind, sir?
Guest : A double room (   ) a fine view.

2

Guest : How about a double room?
Reservation Clerk : No doubles, either.
We have a (   ) house during that period.

3

Guest : Yes, please give me the reservation desk.
Operator : One moment, please. I'll (   ) you with the reservation desk.

4

Reservation Clerk : Would you please tell me the (   ) of your reservation?

Guest : It was for August 15th.

5

Guest : Yes. Could you (   ) me through to Room 3210?

Operator : Certainly, sir. Just a moment, please.
The line's busy. Would you like to hold or call back?

6

Operator : That's 508. What (   ) do you want to call?

Guest : 412-562.

7

Guest : Could you (   ) me up at 4:00, please?

Operator : Yes, sir. What's your room number?

8

Guest : When he returns, could you (   ) him call me?

Operator : Certainly, sir.

Activity

1. *Act out the given situations. One student will be the reservation clerk, the other student will be the guest, and then switch roles after each role-play.*

Guest	: Mr. Youngsik Kim
Room type guest wants	: a double with a good view of the beach and nonsmoking
Room rate	: $100.00/double
Room status	: doubles only
Room features	: air-conditioned, spacious, refrigerator, but no view of beach
Period of stay	: 5 days, February 2nd – 7th

Reservation Form

Guest name : ____________________

Arrival date : ____________________

Number of nights : __________ nights

Smoking : __________ or non-smoking: __________

Room type : single __________, double __________

king __________, queen __________,

twin __________

Room rate : ____________________

Method of payment : __________ Cash

__________ Traveler's Checks

__________ Visa

__________ Master Card

__________ American Express

Card number : ____________________

Expiry date : ____________________

Address : ____________________

Phone number : ____________________

Confirmation number : ____________________

2. ***Act out the given situations. One student will be the telephone operator, the other student will be the guest, and then switch roles after each role-play.***

(1)

Guest	: Mrs. Perkins
Room number	: 815
Request	: Wake-up call at 7:00 a.m.

(2)

Guest	: Mr. Gary Bonhard
Room number	: 2215
Request	: Overseas call to Mr. Smith who lives in Los Angeles, and whose phone number is 456-0432

(3)

Guest	: Mr. John Taylor
Room number	: 725
Request	: collect call to Mr. Brown who lives in Seoul, and whose phone number is 582-4612

(4)

Guest	: Mr. Youngho Kim
Room number	: 4255
Request	: Person to person call to Mrs. Park

Unit 2

Door & Room Services

Introduction to the Job Field

Reading 1: Doorman

When a guest comes to a hotel, the doorman is the first person to welcome that person. The doorman greets visitors, helps them out of the car and opens the hotel door for them. The hotel doormen are usually considered front-desk employees. They usually give the first impression of the hotel to the guests. They are stationed at the entrances to the hotel and help the guests or other visitors in and out of cars and taxis. They also summon taxis or other types of transportation, and in many hotels they carry baggage from the street into the lobby. They may also need to give instructions and directions for reaching local places that the guests wish to visit. All of them wear uniforms while they are on duty.

Reading 2: Room Clerk

The employee who checks in arriving guests and assigns them to their rooms is the room clerk. When the guest arrives, the room clerk checks his reservation or the availability of rooms if the guest does not have a confirmed reservation. When the room clerk has confirmed the availability of the accommodations, the guest fills out a registration card with his name, home address, and any other pertinent information. The room clerk fills in the room number and the rate the guest will pay. One section or a copy of the registration card is normally sent to the cashier's office and another to the telephone switchboard. Another procedure that has come into common practice in recent years is establishing credit in advance by means of credit cards. When the check-in or registration procedure is complete, the room clerk calls a bellman and gives him a slip with the room number. The bellman then gets the room key from the room clerk and escorts the guest to his room.

Reading 3: 10 Ways to Satisfy Customers

Front desk employees handle guests' reservations, registration and check out. In addition to these tasks, front desk employees supervise guest arrivals and departures, and process complaints in all areas. It is also the responsibility of these front desk employees to distribute and forward mail and messages to the appropriate guests and hotel employees.

Here are some ways in which front desk employees can satisfy customers.

(1) Recognize your guest.

(2) Make a positive first impression.

(3) Fulfill your guest's expectations.

(4) Reduce the effort required of the customer.

(5) Facilitate customer decision making.

(6) Focus on the customer's perception.

(7) Avoid violating customer's unspoken time limits.

(8) Create memories customers want to recapture.

(9) Realize your customer to remember bad experience.

(10) Put the customer in your debt.

Prep. for Conversation

Vocabulary 1: Door Service

Match each word in the first column with its meaning in the second column.

(1) revolving door •	• ⓐ 귀중품
(2) valet parking •	• ⓑ 주차장
(3) parking lot •	• ⓒ 주차대행 서비스
(4) valuables •	• ⓓ 회전문
(5) baggage •	• ⓔ 짐

Vocabulary 2: Room Service

Match each word in the first column with its meaning in the second column.

(6) cash •	• ⓕ 예약하지 않고 온 손님
(7) registration card (form) •	• ⓖ 투숙(하다)
(8) bill •	• ⓗ 현금
(9) traveler's check •	• ⓘ 계산서
(10) walk-in guest •	• ⓙ 숙박카드
(11) check-in •	• ⓚ 여행자수표

Key Expressions: Doorman & Check-in

How can you say the following in English?

1. 제가 가방을 안으로 옮겨 드릴까요?

(I, carry, inside, your bags, shall, ?)

2. 앞쪽으로 이동시켜 주십시오.

(forward, please, move)

3. 다음 버스는 약 15분 후에 있습니다.

(the next bus, about, 15 minutes, in, is)

4. 차를 불러 드릴까요?

(your car, I, call, shall, ?)

5. 트렁크에 짐을 실어 드릴까요?

(may, your luggage, the trunk, in, I, put, ?)

6. 체크인 합니다.

(check-in, please, I'd like to)

7. 예약하셨습니까?

(a reservation, you, have, do, ?)

8. 오늘부터 5일 동안 예약이 되어 있습니다.

(today, from, five nights, for, here, a reservation, have, I)

9. 오늘 저녁 객실이 있습니까?

(tonight, for, there, are, rooms, any, available, ?)

10. 등록카드를 작성해 주시겠습니까?

(the registration card, fill out, you, could, please, ?)

Practice Makes Perfect

Conversation 1 Baggage Service

D : Doorman G : Guest

D : Welcome to the Chosun Hotel.

May I help you with your baggage?

G : Yes, please. Don't forget my suitcase in the trunk.

D : Don't worry, sir. I'll take care of everything.

Please watch out for the revolving door.

The inside door is automatic.

G : Thank you. Where can I register?

D : You can register at the front desk right over there on your left.

G : Oh, yes. I see, thanks.

Conversation 2 Baggage Service

D : Doorman G : Guest

D : Good afternoon, ma'am. Welcome to the Lotte Hotel.

G : Thanks. Please take care of my bags.

D : Of course, ma'am.

Just leave them here and our bellman will take care of them.

G : Good. I'll be at the front desk.

Conversation 3 Parking Service

D : Doorman G : Guest

D : Good afternoon.

G : Can you park my car in the parking lot?

D : You can use our hotel's valet parking system.

Someone will take care of everything. Enjoy your stay, sir.

G : Thank you.

D : You're welcome.

Conversation 4 Paging Service

D : Doorman G : Guest

D : Good morning, sir. Are you leaving today?

G : Yes, I'm going to take the one o'clock flight.

D : Are you? Then you'd better hurry to get to the airport on time.

It's almost 11 o'clock.

G : Would you call my car?

D : Certainly, sir. What's the licence number of your car?

G : Seoul 3 GA 2122, Grandeur.

D : Wait a moment, please. I'll call it right away.

Seoul 3 GA 2122 for pick-up, please. Here it comes.

G : I have one more bag, a black bag in front of the bell desk.

Will you bring it to me?

D : Yes sir. I'll put the baggage in your car.

G : Thanks a lot.

Conversation 5 Check–in for Reserved Guests

F : Front Office Clerk G : Guest

F : Good evening, sir. May I help you?

G : My name is John Smith. I have a reservation.

F : Just a moment, Mr. Smith. I'll check the list. Yes, we have your reservation. That was a double room, right?

G : Right.

F : Would you fill out this registration form, please?

G : All right, ... Here you go.

F : Thank you very much. Here is your key. Your room number is 1205. The bellman will show you to your room.

Conversation 6 Check–in for a Walk–in Guest

F : Front Office Clerk G : Guest

F : Good evening. What can I do for you?

G : Do you have any rooms available for tonight?

F : Just a moment, ma'am. How long will you be staying, ma'am?

G : Two nights.

F : What type of room do you want?

G : I'd like to have a single room. How much does it cost per night?

F : 160 U.S. dollars including service charge and tax, ma'am.

G : That's good. I'll take it.

Conversation 7 Dealing with a Reservation Mix-up

Ⓕ : Front Office Clerk Ⓖ : Guest

F : Good evening, sir. May I help you?

G : I booked a double room here for tonight. The name's Wilson.

F : Just a moment, Mr. Wilson.
I'm sorry, but I don't have any record of that.
When was it made?

G : About a couple of weeks ago.

F : From which country?

G : Korea.

F : Who made the reservation?

G : I did.

F : Have you got a letter or telex confirming your booking?

G : No, I haven't.

F : Well, I'm terribly sorry, Mr. Wilson.
There must have been some mistake.
Unfortunately, we're fully booked for this evening.
Would you like me to get you a room in another hotel?

G : Yes, please.

F : Why don't you sit down over there while I take care of it?

G : Thank you.

Conversation 8 Check-in for a Group of Guests

Ⓕ : Front Office Clerk Ⓖ : Guest

F : May I help you, sir?

G : Yes, my name is Changsu Kim.

I'm the escort for the tour group from Korea.

F : Welcome to the Renaissance Hotel, Mr. Kim.

We've been expecting you.

G : I hope our rooms are all ready.

F : Of course, they are, Mr. Kim.

We are holding 15 twins and a single for you.

G : May I see the rooming list?

F : Here you are. Shall I set up a master account for your group, sir?

G : Yes, please. Our baggage will be arriving soon.

It should total 31 pieces.

F : All labeled?

G : Yes. Would you mind having your porter deliver them to each room according to the list?

F : Of course not, Mr. Kim. I hope you will enjoy staying here.

Practice Point

Complete the following conversations relating to the previous Conversations.

1

Doorman : Please, watch out for the (   ) door.
The inside door is automatic.

Guest : Thank you.

2

Doorman : Good afternoon, ma'am. Welcome to the Lotte Hotel.

Guest : Thanks. Please take (   ) of my bags.

3

Guest : Can you (   ) my car in the parking lot?

Doorman : You can use our hotel's valet parking system.

4

Doorman : Good morning, sir. Are you leaving today?

Guest : Yes, I'm going to (   ) the one o'clock flight.

5

Guest	:	All right, ... Here you go.
Front Office Clerk	:	Thank you very much. Here is your key. Your room number is 1205. The bellman will ( ) you to your room.

6

Front Office Clerk	:	What ( ) of room do you want?
Guest	:	I'd like to have a single room.

7

Front Office Clerk	:	Who made the reservation?
Guest	:	I ( ).

8

Guest	:	Yes, my name is Changsu Kim. I'm the ( ) for the tour group from Korea.
Front Office Clerk	:	Welcome to the Renaissance Hotel, Mr. Kim.

Activity

1. *Act out the given situations. One student will be the doorman, the other student will be the guest, and then switch roles after each role-play.*

Number of bags	: two
Requests from the guest	: He wants his baggage taken out of the trunk and to be delivered to the Front.

2. *Act out the given situations. One student will be the room clerk, the other student will be the guest, and then switch roles after each role-play.*

Guest	: Miss Young-mi Kim
Reservation	: No
Room type guest wants	: a double with a good view of the beach
Room rate	: \$80.00/single, \$100.00/twin
Room status	: no doubles, only twins
Room features	: air-conditioned, spacious, refrigerator, cable TV and audio system, mini-bar, a good view of beach
Period of stay	: 3 nights, March 14th – March 17th

Unit 3

Bell & Concierge Services

Introduction to the Job Field

Reading: Bell & Concierge Services

The bell desk is located in the lobby near the front desk. Bellmen provide many services between the guests and the front desk like a messenger. In most large hotels, they work around the clock in shifts. Other terms used for these employees are bellboys and bellhops. In a large hotel, a bell captain is in charge of the bellmen. When the check-in or registration procedure is completed, the room clerk calls a bellman and gives him a slip with the room number. The bellman then gets the room key from the room clerk and escorts the guest to his room. In addition to taking the guests to their rooms, the bellman also shows them where to locate light switches and other equipment. He also shows the guests how to operate air conditioners, television sets, and other appliances in the room. Bellmen are also expected to run errands for the guests, and they should be able to answer questions about other services offered by the hotel such as laundry, dry cleaning, restaurants, and room-service hours.

The hotel concierges take care of problems in the hotel or get you to whom you need for whatever you are asking. They tell you about the town/city you are in. They know a lot about local attractions, tours, secrets, etc. They can recommend everything from a good massage therapist to arranging some tours, etc. for you. They can also get you rental cars, dining arrangements, etc. They just provide a convenient service with the knowledge they are able to provide for the area. Should they meet a customer having a complaint, they must take immediate action without delay, no matter who the customers are, even if it seems trivial.

Prep. for Conversation

Vocabulary: Room Items

Match each word in the first column with its meaning in the second column.

(1) ashtray	•	• ⓐ 옷걸이
(2) hanger	•	• ⓑ 문구류
(3) telephone directory	•	• ⓒ 화장지
(4) stationery	•	• ⓓ 재떨이
(5) pillow	•	• ⓔ 전화번호부
(6) toilet paper	•	• ⓕ 베개
(7) soap	•	• ⓖ 슬리퍼
(8) hair drier	•	• ⓗ 타월
(9) towel	•	• ⓘ 헤어드라이어
(10) slipper	•	• ⓙ 비누

Key Expressions: Bellman & Concierge

How can you say the following in English?

1. 손님 짐을 위해서 카트를 가져오겠습니다.

(I'll, a cart, bring, your baggage, for)

2. 이것이 손님의 짐 전부입니까?

(this, is, your, all, baggage?)

3. 깨질 물건이나 귀중품이 있습니까?

(there, is, breakable, valuable, anything, or, ?)

4. 제가 방까지 안내해드리겠습니다.

(I'll, you, your room, show, to)

5. 늦게 가져와서 죄송합니다.

(I'm, the delay, sorry, for, sir)

6. 짐을 가지고 왔습니다.

(I, your, baggage, brought, have)

7. 짐을 어디에 놓아드릴까요?

(Where, I, your baggage, can, put ?)

8. 서울에서 관광을 좀 하고자 합니다.

....

(I'd like, some sightseeing, do, to, Seoul, in)

9. 백화점이 오전 10시에 문을 엽니다.

....

(The department store, in the morning, 10:00, at, opens)

10. 백화점이 저녁 8시 경에 문을 닫습니다.

....

(The department store, in the evening, closes, 8:00, around)

Practice Makes Perfect

Conversation 1 From the Bell Desk to the Room

B : Bellman G : Guest

B : This way, please.

I'll show you to your room.

The elevator is over there.

G : Thank you.

B : Here, we're on the 15th floor.

Room 1503 is on your left side.

This is your room.

G : It's a very nice room.

B : I'm glad that you like it, sir.

Is there anything else I can do for you, sir?

G : No, I don't think so.

B : Well, if you need any help, please feel free to call the bell desk.

G : I'll do that.

Thank you very much.

Conversation 2 Bringing Baggage to the Room

Ⓑ : Bellman Ⓖ : Guest

G : Who's it?

B : Bell service. I brought your bags.

G : Just a minute. Come on in.

B : Sorry for the delay, sir.

G : That's all right. Leave them there.

B : Is this the correct number of bags?

G : Let's see. Yes, that's all.

B : OK. Enjoy your stay.

Conversation 3 Taking Baggage Down

Ⓑ : Bellman Ⓖ : Guest

B : Good afternoon, Bell Desk. May I help you?

G : Yes, please. I'm going to check out.

Would you take down my luggage?

B : Certainly, sir. Would you tell me your room number, please?

G : 1505 and I'm Robert Bruce.

B : Room 1505.

I'll be there right away, Mr. Bruce.

Conversation 4 Delivery of Bags to the Wrong Room

Ⓑ : Bellman Ⓖ : Guest

B : This is the Bell Desk.

May I help you?

G : Yes, I've been waiting for my bags to be sent up for the last half an hour. Where are they?

B : I'm very sorry to hear that, sir.

May I have your name and room number, please?

G : Yes, it's Simon. Room 1512.

B : How many pieces did you have, ma'am?

G : Two suitcases and a shoulder bag.

B : Could you describe them, please?

G : The suitcases are pale blue Samsonites and the shoulder bag is dark brown.

B : Is there a name tag attached to each of them, sir?

G : Yes, they all have tags on them.

B : We're very sorry for the delay, sir.

I'll check immediately and call you back.

(a while later)

B : This is the bellman.

Your bags are on the way now.

We're very sorry for the inconvenience.

G : How long will it take?

B : About five minutes, sir.

G : I see, all right. Thank you, bye.

B : Good-bye, sir.

Conversation 5 City Information

C : Concierge G : Guest

C : Concierge, may I help you?

G : Yes, I'd like to ask you a question.

C : Sure, go ahead.

G : I'd like to do some sightseeing in Seoul, and I don't know where to go. Would you recommend some good places to visit?

C : Changkyeong Palace will be a nice place to visit, sir.

G : Where is it?

C : It is not far from here. It'll take about 20 minutes by taxi. If you come down here, I'll give you a map of Seoul.

Conversation 6 Shopping Information

C : Concierge G : Guest

C : Good morning. What can I do for you, ma'am?

G : I want to buy some souvenirs for my kids in Korea. Would you please recommend some good places for shopping?

C : First, you can go to the department stores adjoining this hotel. And also, you can try our arcade in the basement.

G : That sounds fantastic! I'll try some department stores this afternoon. By the way, can you tell me what their hours are?

C : Well, they open at ten o'clock in the morning. And they close around eight in the evening.

Conversation 7 Mail Service

C : Concierge G : Guest

G : Miss Kim. Can you help me?

C : Certainly. What can I do for you?

G : Please call DHL. I need to send some documents to my company in LA. But I have an important meeting and I have to rush.

C : Don't worry, sir. You can leave it here, and I will send it by DHL.

G : Thank you. How much do I pay for it?

C : I will transfer it to your room account.

G : Great! Do you know my name and room number?

C : Sure. You are Mr. Richard and your room no. is 1520, right?

G : Yes. Thank you very much for your help.

C : You're welcome. It's my pleasure.

Conversation 8 Helping Restaurant Reservation

C : Concierge G : Guest

G : Can you recommend some places for our dinner?

C : Why don't you have your dinner at the Korean Restaurant?

G : Should I make a reservation?

C : Yes, sir. You had better make a reservation.

G : Will you put me on the reservation list?

C : Yes, sir. May I have your name, please?

G : My name is Thomas Brown.

Practice Point

Complete the following conversations relating to the previous Conversations.

1

Bellman : Well, if you need any help, please feel (　　　　　) to call the bell desk.

Guest : I'll do that.

2

Guest : Who's (　　　　　)?

Bellman : Bell service. I brought your bags.

3

Bellman : Would you tell me your (　　　　　) number, please?

Guest : 1505 and I'm Robert Bruce.

4

Bellman : Is there a name tag attached to each of them, sir?

Guest : Yes, they all have tags (　　　　　) them.

5

Guest : Yes, I'd like to ask you a question.

Concierge : Sure, go (   ).

6

Guest : I want to buy some souvenirs for my kids in Korea. Would you please (   ) some good places for shopping?

Concierge : First, you can go to the department stores adjoining this hotel.

7

Guest : Thank you. How much do I pay for it?

Concierge : I will transfer it to your room (   ).

8

Concierge : Yes, sir. You had better make a reservation.

Guest : Will you put me (   ) the reservation list?

Activity

1. ***Act out the given situations. One student will be the bellman, the other student will be the guest, and then switch roles after each role-play.***

Guest	: Mr. John Jackson
Room number	: 1454
Number of bags	: two
Requests	: He wants his baggage delivered for check-out.
Condition	: He wants two pieces of baggage left at the bell desk for about 3 hours.

2. ***Act out the given situations. One student will be the concierge, the other student will be the guest, and then switch roles after each role-play.***

The guest wants to do some sightseeing in Seoul.
Concierge suggests a city tour.

Unit 4

Housekeeping

Introduction to the Job Field

Reading: Housekeeping Department

The housekeeping department consists of three areas. They are the roommaid service and the laundry service, along with the lost and found service.

The roommaids' duties include making or changing beds, dusting furniture, sweeping or cleaning floors and carpets, washing bathrooms, replacing towels, and supplying the rooms with the items that are specified by management. Heavier chores are performed by men who are usually called housemen. Their work involves window-washing, shampooing carpets, removing and cleaning draperies, cleaning the public areas of the hotel, polishing metal, and many other tasks that might be considered beyond the physical capacities of women. The housemen also run errands for the housekeeping department, such as filling guests' requests for special pillows, extra hangers, cribs for infants, irons, ironing boards, and hair driers.

The biggest part of the hotel's work is the laundry. Laundry service includes washing and valet service includes dry cleaning and pressing. In many hotels, the laundry and valet service take care of the needs of the guests and the hotel itself.

Still another part of the housekeeping job is handling lost and found articles. Guests frequently misplace or leave behind their personal possessions in hotel rooms. These articles usually show up when the room maids make up the room. They are then turned over to the housekeeper who stores them until they are claimed or disposed of in some other way. The housekeeping staff must coordinate its activities closely with the front desk.

Prep. for Conversation

Vocabulary: Housekeeping

Match each word in the first column with its meaning in the second column.

(1) vacuum carpets	•	• ⓐ 침대를 정돈하다
(2) replace towels	•	• ⓑ 금속제품을 광내다
(3) sweep floors	•	• ⓒ 카펫을 진공청소하다
(4) dust furniture	•	• ⓓ 타월을 교체하다
(5) make beds	•	• ⓔ 가구의 먼지를 털다
(6) polish metal	•	• ⓕ 마룻바닥을 쓸다
(7) laundry	•	• ⓖ (세탁물) 특별 서비스
(8) laundry slip	•	• ⓗ (세탁물) 보통 서비스
(9) pressing	•	• ⓘ 얼룩
(10) stain spot	•	• ⓙ 다림질
(11) regular service	•	• ⓚ 세탁표
(12) quick service	•	• ⓛ 세탁소, 세탁물

Key Expressions: Housekeeping

How can you say the following in English?

1. 객실정비입니다. 무엇을 도와드릴까요?

....

(I, help, may, you, housekeeping, ?)

2. 더운물이 나오지 않습니다.

....

(the hot water, working, is, not, faucet)

3. 에어컨이 아직 작동되지 않습니다.

....

(the air conditioner, working, is not, yet)

4. 제방을 청소해 주십시오.

....

(I, cleaned, my room, up, need)

5. 세탁을 할 수 있습니까?

....

(I, some laundry, have, can, done, ?)

6. 세탁물이 무엇입니까?

....

(laundry, kind, what, you, of, do, have, ?)

7. 내일 아침까지 되겠습니다.

....

(they'll, tomorrow morning, be, ready)

8. 세탁물을 가지러 사람을 보내겠습니다.

....

(I'll, your things, have, a valet, up, pick)

9. 저 시계를 잃어버렸습니다.

....

(I, watch, lost, my)

10. 이 "분실신고서"를 작성하여 주십시오.

....

(fill, out, "Lost "Article Report", this, please)

Practice Makes Perfect

Conversation 1 Extra Towel

Ⓗ : Housekeeping Clerk Ⓖ : Guest

H : Housekeeping, may I help you?

G : This is Frank Bennet, room 1109.

I need an extra towel. Can you bring it to me?

H : Certainly, sir. What kind of towel do you need?

G : Ah .... face towel, please.

H : All right, I'll send someone with a towel right away.

G : Thanks a lot.

Conversation 2 Heating Controller

Ⓗ : Housekeeping Clerk Ⓖ : Guest

G : May I speak to the floor supervisor, please?

H : Yes, speaking.

G : I think the room is not warm enough. I'm worried I might catch a cold.

H : There is a heating controller on the wall. Is it properly adjusted?

G : I know how to handle the controller.

It's still cold even though I adjusted it to the highest point.

H : It seems something must be wrong with it. What's your room number?

We'll call the maintenance immediately and have it fixed for you.

Conversation 3 Pick Up the Laundry

Ⓛ : Laundry Clerk Ⓖ : Guest

L : Laundry service, may I help you?

G : Yes, I have some shirts to be cleaned and pressed.

Can you send someone to my room?

L : May I have your name and room number, please?

G : My name is Frank Bennet, and my room number is 1516.

L : All right, sir. I'll have a valet pick them up right away.

G : All right. Thank you.

Conversation 4 No Starch

Ⓛ : Laundry Clerk Ⓖ : Guest

L : Laundry service. May I come in?

G : Yes, I'd like to have this laundry done, please.

L : Certainly, sir. Could you fill out the laundry form, please?

G : Where is it?

L : It's in the drawer of the writing desk.

G : Fine, may I use your pen?

L : Certainly, sir. Here you are.

G : Thanks. Oh, I don't want these shirts starched.

L : No starch, I understand, sir.

G : Yes, and I'd like this sweater washed by hand in cold water.

Otherwise, it might shrink.

L : By hand in cold water. Certainly, sir.

Conversation 5 Describe Your Lost One

Ⓛ : Lost & Found Clerk Ⓖ : Guest

G : Pardon, me, Miss ....

L : Yes, ma'am, may I help you?

G : I think I've lost my purse.

Might it be in your lost and found section?

L : Well, I can check, ma'am.

What is your purse made of and what color is it?

G : It's made of leather and is beige.

My name is printed on it.

L : Just a minute, ma'am ....

I'm sorry, but I'm afraid we don't have any purses at all.

Are you sure you didn't leave it in your room?

G : Yes, I looked all over for it in my room, and it's not there.

L : Where did you go shopping, ma'am?

G : At the hotel shopping arcade.

L : Don't worry, ma'am.

Please fill out this lost article report and I'll make sure to contact you if it's found.

Practice Point

Complete the following conversations relating to the previous Conversations.

1

Housekeeping Clerk : Housekeeping, may I help you?

Guest : (   ) is Frank Bennet, room 109.

2

Guest : It's still cold even though I adjusted it to the highest point.

Housekeeping Clerk : It seems something must be wrong with it. What's your room number? We'll call the maintenance immediately and have it (   ) for you.

3

Guest : Can you send someone to my room?

Laundry Clerk : May I have your name and (   ) number, please?

4

Lost & Found Clerk : Yes, ma'am, may I help you?

Guest : I think I've lost my purse. Might it be in your lost and (   ) section?

5

Lost & Found Clerk : Where did you go shopping, ma'am?

Guest : At the hotel (   ) arcade.

Activity

1. *Act out the given situations. One student will be the room maid, the other student will be the guest, and then switch roles after each role-play.*

Guest	: Ms. Jane Cox
Room Number	: 1015
Room Features	: no bath towels, room maid didn't make up the room

2. *Act out the given situations. One student will be the laundry clerk, the other student will be the guest, and then switch roles after each role-play.*

Room number of the guest	: 1150
Requirement of the guest	: The guest wants a shirt pressed and a suit dry cleaned as soon as possible.

3. *Act out the given situations. One student will be the lost and found clerk, the other student will be the guest, and then switch roles after each role-play.*

Lost item	: a wallet which is made of leather, whose brand is Pierre Carding and whose color is red.
Last Known Location	: Coffee shop on the first floor
Date Missing	: July 27

Unit 5

Room Service

Introduction to the Job Field

Reading: Room Service

Room Service is a service provided by a hotel for food, drink and services which are delivered or carried out in person's room. A hotel lodger can receive room service by phone or prior scheduling. Most room service is for food, so it usually belongs to the Food & Beverage Division. It differs from the room-related department, such as the front desk and house keeping sections which are responsible for room cleaning, maintenance, and laundry service.

Room service is a food delivery system. The right food should be delivered in the right room at the right time. The key people in room service are the order taker, the waiter and the cook. The order taker writes the guest's order accurately. The waiter sees that the guest's wishes are carried out. The cook cooperates with the waiter by preparing the food on time.

Prep. for Conversation

Vocabulary: Tea & Toast

Match each word in the first column with its meaning in the second column.

*Tea

(1) black tea	•	• ⓐ 녹차
(2) green tea	•	• ⓑ 자스민(중국차)
(3) jasmin tea	•	• ⓒ 우롱차(중국차)
(4) oolong	•	• ⓓ 홍차

*Toast

Toast is ___________.

(5) dark	•	• ⓔ 덜 구웠습니다.
(6) light	•	• ⓕ 많이 구웠습니다.
(7) burnt	•	• ⓖ 탔습니다.
(8) stale	•	• ⓗ 물렁물렁합니다.
(9) damp	•	• ⓘ 축축합니다.
(10) soggy	•	• ⓙ 오래된 것 같습니다.

Key Expressions: Room Service

How can you say the following in English?

1. 여보세요. 여기 677호실인데요.

(Hello, this, 677, room, is)

2. 아침식사 1인분을 주문하고 싶습니다.

(I, breakfast, one, for, order, to, want)

3. 저희 룸서비스는 한식, 중식, 일식, 아메리칸식 식사가 가능합니다.

(We, food, Korean, Chinese, Japanese, American, and, have)

4. 우리가 여기서 간단한 파티를 열려고 하는데 마실 것과 과자 좀 갖다 줬으면 합니다.

(We're going to, here, a little, party, you, want, deliver, to, some drinks and snacks, and, have)

5. 맥주와 프레첼을 올려 보내주시겠습니까?

(some beer, pretzels, and, you, up, send, would, ?)

6. 주문하신 음식을 몇 시에 갖다 드릴까요?

(your meal, what time, you, like, would, ?)

7. 네, 선생님, 한 30분 내에 올려 보내드리겠습니다.

(OK, sir, we'll, 30 minutes, in, up, it, send, about)

8. 음식이 10분 후에 제공될 것입니다.

....

(Your food, 10, minutes, in, served, be, about, will)

9. 잠시 후에 웨이터가 갈 것입니다.

....

(seconds, there, up, be, will, a waiter, in)

10. 주문해 주셔서 감사합니다.

....

(your order, thank, for, you)

Practice Makes Perfect

Conversation 1 Breakfast Service

G : Guest R : Room Service

R : Room service, may I help you, sir?

G : Yes, please. I'd like to have breakfast in my room.

R : What would you like to have, sir?

G : I'd like two eggs, toast, a grilled sausage, and coffee.

R : How would you like your eggs?

G : Scrambled, please.

R : May I have your name and room number?

G : Yes. This is Frank Lewis in room 907.

R : What else would you like, Mr. Lewis?

G : Bring me some ice water, please. How long will it take?

R : It'll take about 20 minutes.

G : Okay. I have an appointment with my friend. I don't have much time. Please bring it as soon as possible.

R : Yes. Thank you for using room service, Mr. Lewis.

Conversation 2 Beverage Service

Ⓖ : Guest Ⓡ : Room Service

R : Good afternoon, room service. What can I help you with, sir?

G : We'd like to have a cup of coffee and some juice.

R : What kind of coffee and juice do you want, sir?

G : Irish coffee and tomato juice, please.

R : What's your room number, sir?

G : Room 615.

R : Is there anything else, sir?

G : That's all.

R : Your order will be served in about 15 minutes. Thank you for your order, sir.

Conversation 3 Breakfast Service

Ⓖ : Guest Ⓡ : Room Service

G : Who is it?

R : It's room service. May I come in?

G : Come right in, please.

R : Good morning, Mr. Brown.
I've brought your breakfast order.
Where shall I put it?

G : Please put it on the table by the window.

R : Shall I pour the coffee now, Mr. Brown?

G : Yes, please.

R : I've brought you a newspaper to read at breakfast.

Here you are.

G : It's very kind of you to do this service.

R : It's our pleasure. Do you want to have something else, Mr. Brown?

G : No, that's okay. Will you charge it to the room?

R : Certainly, sir. Please call room service anytime if you need anything else. We're always ready for you.

G : Oh, yes.

R : Would you please sign this slip, Mr. Brown?

G : Sure. Here it is.

R : And this is for you. Please enjoy your breakfast, Mr. Brown.

Conversation 4 Dinner Service

Ⓖ : Guest Ⓡ : Room Service

R : (Knocking on the door) Room service!

G : Come in.

R : Good evening, sir. I've brought the dinner you ordered. Where would you like to eat?

G : Over there by the window.

R : All right, sir. Here you are, porterhouse steak and a bottle of wine. Would you like me to pour the wine now, sir?

G : Yes, please.

R : Will there be anything else, sir?

G : No, I think this is all ... Oh! Just a moment.

R : Yes, sir.

G : This here is potato soup. But I am sure that I ordered cream of mushroom.

R : Oh, I'm sorry, sir. The reception clerk must have misunderstood you. I'll bring you cream of mushroom soup immediately.

G : Yeah, please make it quick! I'm very hungry.

R : I'll be right back. (Five minutes later)

Here's your cream of mushroom soup, sir, and we're sorry for the mistake.

It won't happen again.

G : That's all right. Here, this is for you.

R : No, thank you, sir, we have a "no tipping" policy here. But there will be a ten percent service charge on your bill.

G : OK, that's fine.

R : Thanks anyway, sir. Enjoy your dinner.

Practice Point

Complete the following conversations relating to the previous Conversations.

1

Room Service : ( ) would you like your eggs?

Guest : Scrambled, please.

2

Room Service : What's your ( ) number, sir?

Guest : Room 615.

3

Guest : Who is ( )?

Room Service : It's room service. May I come in?

4

Room Service : All right, sir. Here you are, porterhouse steak and a bottle of wine. Would you like me to ( ) the wine now, sir?

Guest : Yes, please.

Activity

1. ***Act out the given situations. One student will be the room service clerk, the other student will be the guest, and then switch roles after each role-play.***

Mr. Johnson is in room 907.

He wants to have breakfast in his room.

He wants a scrambled egg, toast, and coffee.

He wants his breakfast as soon as possible.

Unit 6

Leisure & Others

Introduction to the Job Field

Reading 1: Comprehensive Services

A hotel is a temporary home for people who are traveling. In a hotel the traveler can rest and has access to food and drink, either on the premises or nearby. The hotel may also offer facilities for recreation, such as a swimming pool, a golf course, or a beach.

In large cities that are also tourist centers, such as New York, Paris, London, Rome and Tokyo, one hotel may offer all types of service. And even a small motel may have banquet rooms, and meeting rooms in addition to its accommodations for transients. Many resort hotels nowadays are also designed with complete convention facilities.

Comprehensive Service

Beauty Salon and Barber Shop

The hotel provides expert hair-dressing, facial treatment & massage, and other services.

Business Center

The Business Center offers typing, copying, faxing, computer rental, internet service, meeting room rental and postal service.

Recreation Center

The Recreation Center includes an in-door swimming pool, sauna, steam bath, gymnasium, billiard room, video-game room, and garaoke singing-dancing hall.

Shopping Arcade

The shopping arcades are on the ground floor.

Reading 2: Check-out Procedure

Like the check-in procedure, it takes only a few moments, when the system works efficiently, for a guest to settle his bill. The front desk clerk receives the key and checks to see if there are any extra charges owed for phone calls, movies, food, or other services. If there is an outstanding bill, the front desk clerk must present the bill to the guest. After the bill is paid, the doorman helps the guest with his baggage and assists him into his car, a taxi, or one of the hotel's shuttle vans.

Many hotels have a check-out time. If the guest occupies his room beyond that time, he can be charged for an extra day or at least a fraction of a day. The check-out time is usually set between noon and three o'clock in the afternoon to give sufficient time to clean and prepare the rooms for incoming guests. Many commercial hotels receive a large number of guests in the late afternoon or early evening, between four o'clock and eight o'clock. This is often a result of a heavy concentration of arriving airline flights during those hours.

Prep. for Conversation

Vocabulary 1: Leisure

Match each word in the first column with its meaning in the second column.

(1) gym	•	•	ⓐ 기념품가게
(2) souvenir shop	•	•	ⓑ 체육관
(3) golf driving range	•	•	ⓒ 골프채
(4) athletic wear	•	•	ⓓ 운동복
(5) golf club	•	•	ⓔ 골프연습장

Vocabulary 2: Check-out

Match each word in the first column with its meaning in the second column.

(6) check out	•	•	ⓕ 신용카드
(7) guest folio	•	•	ⓖ 서명
(8) credit card	•	•	ⓗ 퇴실
(9) extra charge	•	•	ⓘ 초과요금
(10) signature	•	•	ⓙ 고객원장(guest bill)

Key Expressions: Leisure

How can you say the following in English?

1. 호텔 내에 이발관이 있습니다까?

(the hotel, in, a barber shop, there, is, ?)

2. 도시 지도를 구할 수 있습니까?

(a city, map, I, can, get, ?)

3. 나이트클럽에 관한 정보를 알 수 있습니까?

(the night club, about, the information, I, may, have, ?)

4. 머리를 어떻게 해드릴까요?

(you, your hair, how, would, done, like, ?)

5. 언제 마지막으로 머리를 잘랐어요?

(when, your hair, done, have, last, did, you, ?)

6. 머리를 다듬어 주세요.

(my hair, want, get, I, to, trimmed)

7. 파마머리를 해주세요.

(a permanent, want, get, I to)

8. 몇 호실 손님입니까?

....

(is, what, room number, your, ?)

9. 오늘 Mini bar에서 드신 것 있으십니까?

....

(today, you, have, anything, minibar, from, did, ?)

10. 가방을 벨 데스크에 보관해 드릴까요?

....

(your bag, the bell, desk, at, keep, may, I)

Practice Makes Perfect

Conversation 1 Fitness Center

F : Fitness Center Clerk G : Guest

F : Good afternoon. How are you, sir?

G : Very good. I am a guest in room 1212. May I use the fitness center?

F : Certainly, would you sign in here, please?

G : Sure. What facilities do you have in your fitness center?

F : We have a fully equipped gym, indoor and outdoor swimming pools, golf driving range, and men's and women's spring water sauna.

G : That sounds great. I want to practice golf swings.
Can I rent golf clubs and shoes?

F : Yes, you can.
We rent golf clubs and shoes for 5,000 won and you get about 100 balls for 2,000 won.

G : Here is 7,000 won.

F : Thank you, sir. Here is your coupon and locker key.
The locker room is on the 2nd floor.
Please exchange your clothes for athletic wear.
The golf range is on the 4th floor. Please show this coupon to the counter.
She will give you golf club, shoes, and balls.

Enjoy!

G : Thank you.

Conversation 2 Gift Shop

S : Sales Clerk G : Guest

S : Can I help you, sir?

G : I need to buy gifts for my children.
What do you recommend?

S : These 2002 World Cup T-shirts are very popular with children.

G : I'll take one small and one medium.

S : Would you like them gift-wrapped?

G : Yes, please. How much are they?

S : They are 15,000 won each. The total is 30,000 won.

G : Here you are.

S : Thank you. Here is your receipt.
Please wait a moment. I'll wrap these.

Conversation 3 Barber Shop

B : Barber G : Guest

B : Good afternoon. How are you, sir?

G : Fine.

B : What can I do for you?

G : I want to get my hair trimmed, so don't cut off too much.

B : I see. Do you want your hair shampooed?

G : Yes, please. And a shave also, please.

B : Sure. Sit back and relax, please.

Conversation 4 Beauty Shop

Ⓗ : Hair Stylist Ⓖ : Guest

H : How are you, ma'am?

Would you like your hair cut?

G : Yes, please. I want to get a hair cut and permanent.

H : How would you like it done?

G : I want a natural wave. Don't make it too curly.

H : I see. When did you have your hair done last?

G : I got a permanent about two months ago.

H : If you want, we provide nail-polishing service.

G : Sure, please.

Conversation 5 Paying with A Credit Card

Ⓕ : Front Office Clerk Ⓖ : Guest

F : Good morning, sir.

May I help you?

G : Yes.

I'm checking-out. Here is my room key.

I'd like to take care of my bill.

F : Cash or credit card?

G : I'd like to pay for that with my credit card.

F : Yes, sir. Please sign here.

G : OK.

Here it is.

F : Thank you.

Did you enjoy your stay at our hotel?

G : Sure.

I'll come here again when I visit this country.

Conversation 6 Paying with Traveler's Checks

Ⓕ : Front Office Clerk Ⓖ : Guest

G : I'd like to check-out.

How much is the charge?

F : What's your name and room number?

G : I'm Peter Andrew and my room number is 125.

F : Just a minute, sir.

Your bill comes to 250 dollars including the tax and service charge.

G : Can I pay you with a traveler's check?

F : That'll be okay.

G : It's been a very pleasant stay.

F : Thank you for staying with us.

I hope you'll come again.

G : I'll try.

Good-bye.

Conversation 7 Wrong Bill

F : Front Office Clerk G : Guest

G : I'd like to check out now, room 5042.

F : Certainly, sir.

I'll get your bill ....

Here you are.

Here is the guest folio and summary.

Would you like to check if everything is correct?

G : This charge is wrong.

I didn't make an overseas call, but it's on the bill.

F : We're very sorry, Mr. Jackson.

There must be a mistake.

I'll check it through, and prepare a new bill.

Sorry for the inconvenience, Mr. Jackson.

G : OK.

Conversation 8 Extending Check-out Time

F : Front Office Clerk G : Guest

G : Excuse me. Sorry to bother you, but I wonder if you can do me a favor.

F : Sure if I can.

G : My flight doesn't leave until five o'clock this afternoon.

Is there any chance of extending check-out time for me?

F : We're very busy today, but I can give you two extra hours.

Will that help?

G : That's a big help.

Thank you very much.

Practice Point

Complete the following conversations relating to the previous Conversations.

1

Fitness Center Clerk : We have a fully equipped gym, indoor and outdoor swimming pools, golf driving (   ), and men's and women's spring water sauna.

Guest : That sounds great. I want to practice golf swings.

2

Guest : Yes, please. How much are they?

Sales Clerk : They are 15,000 won (   ). The total is 30,000.

3

Barber : What can I do for you?

Guest : I want to get my hair (   ), so don't cut off too much.

4

Hair Stylist : How would you like it done?

Guest : I want a natural wave. Don't make it too (   ).

5

Front Office Clerk : (   ) or credit card?

Guest : I'd like to pay for that with my credit card.

6

Front Office Clerk : Just a minute, sir. Your bill comes to 250 dollars including the tax and service (   ).

Guest : Can I pay you with a traveler's check?

7

Guest : I didn't make an overseas call, but it's (   ) the bill.

Front Office Clerk : We're very sorry, Mr. Jackson.

8

Guest : Excuse me. Sorry to bother you, but I wonder if you can do me a (   ).

Front Office Clerk : Sure if I can.

Activity

1. *Act out the given situations. One student will be the fitness center clerk, the other student will be the guest, and then switch roles after each role-play.*

The guest wants to practice golf swings
The locker room is on the 3rd floor.
The golf range is on the 4th floor.

Golf clubs rental : 5,000 won
Golf shoes rental : 5,000 won
Golf balls rental : 100 balls for 2,000 won

2. *Act out the given situations. One student will be the hotel clerk and the other the guest checking out, and then switch roles after each role-play.*

Guest : Ms. Jennifer Lalonde
Room no. : 1003
Length of stay : six days
Payment style : credit card
Extra charges : telephone bills–$20
laundry–$15
breakfast (2 days)–$20
Check–out time : 1:30 pm
Total charge : $580

REFERENCES

성명희(2006). English for Hotel and Restaurant Services. 서울: 백산출판사.

신재영 외 4인(1997). 호텔 레스토랑 실무영어. 서울: 백산출판사.

양혜순(2001). 관광영어. 서울: 기문사.

여형구 · 정홍진(1998). 관광실무영어. 서울: 기문사.

정중훈(1998). 호텔실무영어. 서울: 학문출판.

조응래(2002). 관광실무영어회화. 서울: 한올출판사.

조춘봉 · 황인태(2001). English for Hotel & Restaurant Services. 서울: 학문사.

http://www.wikipedia.org

http://kr.hotels.com

http://hotels4u.com

http://www.hotelenglish.net

http://www.englishclub.english-for-work/hotel.htm

Answer Key

[CHAPTER_1]

Unit 1

Key Expressions: Reservations & Seating the Guest

1. I'd like to reserve a table for 6.
2. It's good to make your reservation at least one day in advance.
3. In what name shall I make the reservation?
4. I'm sorry. We're fully booked.
5. I want a table by the window.
6. Do you have a reservation?
7. How long of a wait is there?
8. There are about ten minutes to wait.
9. I'll call you when your table is ready.
10. How do you like this table?

Practice Point

1. book, for
2. ready
3. made
4. serve
5. open
6. available, waiting
7. That
8. many
9. chance

Unit 2

Key Expressions: Hotel Breakfast & Lunch Services

1. May I take your order now?
2. What's good on the menu this morning?
3. How would you like your toast, dark or light?
4. Please rush my order. I don't have much time.
5. How would you like your eggs?
6. Spaghetti is not on the menu.
7. The carrots are not cooked enough.
8. What would you like to start with?
9. And what would you like to follow?
10. What would you like for dessert?

Practice Point

1. How	2. accompany	3. Korean
4. with	5. cream	6. hold
7. How	8. ready	9. same

Unit 3

Key Expressions: Dinner Service

1. How would you like (to have) your steak?
2. Did you find your steak all right?
3. This steak is a little bit overdone (undercooked).
4. It's grilled over a charcoal fire.

5. What's happened to my order?
6. I'm sorry to have kept you waiting.
7. Your order will be here in a minute.
8. Will you have them with your dinner?
9. I'll have it cooked some more for you.
10. I'd like to recommend the Caesar salad.

Practice Point

1. French 2. comes 3. with 4. day

Unit 4

Key Expressions: Korean Food Service

1. Bulgogi is one of the most popular Korean dishes among foreigners.
2. What's traditional Korean liquor?
3. We're not sure which to choose.
4. Hanjeongsik consists of a bowl of rice and soup with many side dishes.
5. Broiled fish is also served.
6. Bring two bottles of beer, please.
7. Enjoy your meal, please.
8. I'll bring some right away.
9. It'll take a while to cook.
10. Would you mind waiting, please?

Practice Point

1. bottle 2. take 3. waiting

4. mild 5. keep 6. credit
7. rate 8. charge 9. wrong

Unit 5

Key Expressions: Banquet Service

1. Let's get a podium and a microphone for speakers.
2. Is the lighting and air-conditioning working properly?
3. What to follow?
4. Can I substitute some kind of chicken for the salmon?
5. We will be able to substitute the cornish hen for the salmon.
6. The usual drinks can be arranged?
7. That would leave plenty of space for a little bar to be set up.
8. I'd like you to arrange the drinks.
9. You could send an estimate to my secretary.
10. The menu cost would be about 25 francs per head.

Practice Point

1. many 2. know 3. take 4. furnished

Unit 6

Key Expressions: Coffee Shop & Bar Service

1. How would you like your coffee, please?
2. Would you like some more coffee?
3. Have bacon cooked very crisp, please.

4. Would you care for something to drink?

5. Water will be fine.

6. This is not what I ordered.

7. I asked for draught beer, not bottled beer.

8. I didn't order another drink.

9. This is on the house.

10. A 10% service charge is included.

Practice Point

1. take	2. over	3. cooked
4. fruit	5. dressings	6. recommend
7. brand	8. on	9. side
10. How	11. sweet	

[CHAPTER_2]

Unit 1

Key Expressions: Room Reservations & Telephone

1. When would you like to make your reservation, sir?

2. How long would you like to stay?

3. What tipe of room would you like?

4. I'm afraid there's no vacancy.

5. I'd like a room with a nice view.

6. What is the daily rate?

7. Sorry, but Mr. Johnson is on the line.

8. Shall I have him call you back?

9. There is no one here by that name.

10. Would you hold the line, please?

Practice Point

1. with
2. full
3. connect
4. date
5. put
6. number
7. wake
8. have

Unit 2

Key Expressions: Doorman & Check-in

1. Shall I carry your bags inside?
2. Please move forward.
3. The next bus is in about 15 minutes.
4. Shall I call your car?
5. May I put your luggage in the trunk?
6. I' d like to check-in, please.
7. Do you have a reservation (with us)?
8. I have a reservation for five nights from today.
9. Are there any rooms available for tonight?
10. Could you fill out the registration card, please?

Practice Point

1. revolving
2. care
3. park
4. take
5. take
6. type

7. did

8. escort

Unit 3

Key Expressions: Bellman & Concierge

1. I'll bring a cart for your baggage.
2. Is this all your baggage?
3. Is there anything breakable or valuable?
4. I'll show you to your room.
5. I'm sorry for the delay, sir.
6. I have brought your baggage.
7. Where can I put your baggage?
8. I'd like to do some sightseeing in Seoul.
9. The department store opens at 10:00 in the morning.
10. The department store closes around 8:00 in the evening.

Practice Point

1. free
2. it
3. room
4. on
5. ahead
6. recommend
7. account
8. on

Unit 4

Key Expressions: Housekeeping

1. Housekeeping. May I help you?
2. The hot water faucet is not working.

3. The air conditioner is not working yet.

4. I need my room cleaned up.

5. Can I have some laundry done?

6. What kind of laundry do you have?

7. They'll be ready tomorrow morning.

8. I'll have a valet pick up your things.

9. I lost my watch.

10. Please fill out this "Lost Article Report."

Practice Point

1. This
2. fixed
3. room
4. found
5. shopping

Unit 5

Key Expressions: Room Service

1. Hello, this is room six seventy-seven (677).

2. I want to order breakfast for one.

3. We have Korean, Chinese, Japanese and American food.

4. We're going to have a little party here, and want you to deliver some drinks and snacks.

5. Would you send up some beer and pretzels?

6. What time would you like your meal?

7. OK, sir, we'll send it up in about 30 minutes.

8. Your food will be served in about 10 minutes.

9. A waiter will be up there in seconds.

10. Thank you for your order.

Practice Point

1. How 2. room 3. it 4. pour

Unit 6

Key Expressions: Leisure

1. Is there a barber shop in the hotel?
2. Can I get a city map?
3. May I have the information about the night club?
4. How would you like your hair done?
5. When did you have your hair done last?
6. I want to get my hair trimmed.
7. I want to get a permanent.
8. What is your room number?
9. Did you have anything from the minibar today?
10. May I keep your bag at the bell desk?

Practice Point

1. range 2. each 3. trimmed
4. curly 5. cash 6. charge
7. on 8. favor

저자약력

성명희(Myeong-Hee Seong)

・고려대학교대학원 문학박사
・을지대학교 교수

Practical Restaurant & Hotel English

2010년 12월 31일 초 판 1쇄 발행
2017년 1월 15일 수정판 1쇄 발행

지은이 성명희
펴낸이 진욱상
펴낸곳 백산출판사
교 정 편집부
본문디자인 편집부
표지디자인 오정은

저자와의 합의하에 인지첩부 생략

등 록 1974년 1월 9일 제1-72호
주 소 경기도 파주시 회동길 370(백산빌딩 3층)
전 화 02-914-1621(代)
팩 스 031-955-9911
이메일 edit@ibaeksan.kr
홈페이지 www.ibaeksan.kr

ISBN 978-89-6183-411-7
값 14,000원

• 파본은 구입하신 서점에서 교환해 드립니다.
• 저작권법에 의해 보호를 받는 저작물이므로 무단전재와 복제를 금합니다.
이를 위반시 5년 이하의 징역 또는 5천만원 이하의 벌금에 처하거나 이를 병과할 수 있습니다.